THE COMPLETE GUIDE TO LABRADOODLES

Dr. Jo de Klerk

LP Media Inc. Publishing

Text copyright © 2019 by LP Media Inc.

www.lpmedia.org

Publication Data

Dr. Jo de Klerk

The Complete Guide to Labradoodles ---- First edition.

Summary: "Successfully raising a Labradoodle dog from puppy to old age" --- Provided by publisher.

ISBN: 978-1-69384-7-738

[1. Labradoodles --- Non-Fiction] I. Title.

Design by Sorin Rădulescu

First paperback edition, 2019

TABLE OF CONTENTS

CHAPTER 1
Origins and History

With its shaggy-dog appeal, ebullient nature, friendliness, intelligence, and huge personality, it's hard to believe that one of the world's most popular dogs, the Labradoodle, has only been around since 1989. This sweet-natured ball of fun has so quickly become ingrained in the world's affections that few would realize the Labradoodle is still very much the new kid on the block. And with this relatively new status comes a whole raft of unique factors that anyone considering welcoming a Labradoodle into their life should consider, over and above any long-established breed.

Wally Conron's Story

Although Poodle crossbreeds have been bred on a casual basis throughout the twentieth century and beyond, the man credited with creating the first intentional Labrador Poodle cross for a specific purpose was Wally Conron, who at the time was the puppy breeding manager for the Royal Guide Dog Association of Australia.

FUN FACT
Australian Labradoodle Club of America (ALCA)

The Australian Labradoodle Club of America (ALCA) aims to connect Australian Labradoodle breeders across America, as well as defend the interests of the breed. Since Labradoodles are not a recognized breed under the American Kennel Club, this is not an official club. The club was founded in 2005 by Gail Widman and hopes to help the breed become recognized as a "purebred" breed. For more information about the club, services offered, and membership options, visit the ALCA website at www.australian-labradoodleclub.us

Wally Conron was experienced in producing mainly Labrador and Retriever dogs to be trained as guide dogs, but in the late 1980s he faced a challenge. A blind lady in Hawaii required a guide dog, but her husband had a dog allergy and could not have a profusely shedding Labrador Retriever in the house. Wally turned his attention to a breed of dog known to be mostly hypoallergenic, the Standard Poodle. However, despite his best efforts, the stubborn Poodle proved impossible to train as a guide dog. What was required was the trainability of the Labrador and the hypoallergenic coat

Photo Courtesy of
Jessica Gerrin

of the Poodle. In desperation, Wally bred a male Poodle to a female Labrador, and the first litter of Labrador Poodle crossbreeds was born. In fact, of these three pups, only one turned out not to trigger an allergic reaction in the blind lady's husband. However, it was a promising breakthrough in the problem of supplying service dogs where someone in the household has an allergy.

Unfortunately for the breeding program, Wally immediately came up against a problem with his new miracle pups, and that was that none of the families involved in fostering and training guide dogs wanted to take on a crossbreed. So Wally needed to get on the PR bandwagon, and in a flash of inspiration, he created the name Labradoodle to introduce the Labrador Poodle cross as a new breed. The response was overwhelming, and suddenly everyone wanted the new wonder dog!

Photo Courtesy of
Nicole Grullon Garcia

Early Years

Wally's problems were not over with the new breed of Labradoodle. In the early years, the breed was a simple hybrid, the result of simply crossing a Labrador and a Poodle, and consequently the results were far from predictable. Even within the same litter, the pups could have a variety of coat types, from the copiously shedding 'hair' coat, to the intermediate wavy 'fleece' coat, or the curly but high-maintenance poodle-like 'wool' coat. And without testing the individual puppies, it was impossible to say which, if any, would prove to be hypoallergenic. Plus, with the coat changes that commonly occur at around 6-8 months, a newborn pup might not be a true representation of the qualities he would possess as an adult dog.

Wally also continued to encounter resistance from the Kennel Club in the creation of this new breed, as very few breeders of quality registered Standard Poodles would lend their stud dogs to the program, and those who did insisted on doing so anonymously.

The requirement for purebred Poodle stud dogs, and variability within the litter, was partly addressed as Labradoodles were subsequently bred to other Labradoodles, rather than the initial Labrador Poodle cross, but still each litter remained a lottery. However, Wally Conron's meticulously careful breeding program ensured that only the very best parents were chosen for mating, with both animals screened and tested for genetic conditions, and possessing the best temperaments. Wally nicknamed his second-generation Labradoodles Doubledoodles, and the subsequent generation were the Tripledoodles. However, he only ever bred 31 Labradoodles for the Royal Guide Dogs (29 of which became trained service dogs). There were several reasons for this. In the course of his work, Wally came up against intense opposition from the Kennel Club and those associated with it; the only purpose for which the Labradoodle had been created was to address a specific need for hypoallergenic dogs in households requiring guide dogs, and Wally's heart really lay with Labrador Retrievers. So eventually Wally retired without having achieved registration of the Labradoodle with the Kennel Club, a situation that still exists today.

But sadly, a more sinister reason exists behind Wally Conron's decision to turn his back on the breed that he created, and that is his personal belief that the success of his PR created a "Frankenstein's Monster." He soon observed that every unscrupulous backyard breeder was quick to jump on the Labradoodle craze when they realized how much money could be made in producing the new designer wonder dog that everyone wanted, with the

Photo Courtesy of
Courtney Brock

funky name and non-shedding, hypoallergenic coat with no odor. The Lab-radoodle had become a license to print money.

It is important for every potential owner of a Labradoodle to recognize that careful selection of your new Labradoodle is vitally important. This is not only because you want a healthy and sweet-natured pet to share many happy years with, but you do not want to inadvertently encourage the kind of moneymaking that sullies the breed and creates misery for the poorly bred puppies farmed in this way by backyard breeders. Unfortunately, for as long as the Labradoodle remains an unregistered breed, the checks and balances imposed on Kennel Club–registered breeders to ensure that only the healthiest parents are bred from, and that the pups are raised in suit-able conditions, will only exist on a self-imposed basis.

Fortunately, there are many responsible breeders worldwide who have taken the Labradoodle to heart, and are committed to producing healthy, happy, even-tempered family dogs with all the positive qualities a Labra-doodle should represent. These breeders only raise a small number of lit-ters per year in order to properly rear and socialize their pups, and they will go above and beyond the standard health tests for parents and puppies, in-vesting in their breeding stock, and the future of all the puppies that repre-sent their kennel name. However, it is the job of prospective owners to look carefully at any breeder, no matter how well established, to be sure of their ethics and welfare standards.

There still exists a very wide variation in the breed both between and within countries. For example, the Australian Labradoodle has progressed a long way from the original Labrador Poodle cross. Australian Labradoo-dles are now multigenerational and many also contain the genetics of oth-er breeds such as the Irish Water Spaniel and even the Afghan Hound. But in refining the breed by selective line-breeding, the Australian Labradoodle Club has been able to produce the first breed standard to promote consis-tency going forward.

In America and the UK, Labradoodles are still generally straight Labra-dor Poodle crossbreeds. However, further variations have been produced by varying the size of Poodle used in the mating process, so that Labradoo-dles are no longer necessarily large dogs. This can make the breed very at-tractive to homes where coping with a large breed would be impractical. Labradoodles also come in a wide variety of coat colors, in addition to the three textures: hair, fleece, and wool coat.

Many believe that in keeping as near to the original hybrid cross as pos-sible, the dogs produced are healthier, although the results are less predict-able. For this reason, anyone with an allergy to dogs should not assume that

Photo Courtesy of Krystal Morley

a Labradoodle is hypoallergenic, but should spend a day with the breeder to discover whether his dogs produce a reaction. 'Hypoallergenic,' 'non-shedding,' and 'no odor' continue to be false marketing claims. No dog is fully hypoallergenic, regardless of breed, though some, like Labradoodles, are better than others for people with allergies.

One thing, however, that should be consistent with the breed is the Labradoodle's affectionate, even temperament. Well-bred Labradoodles will never be aggressive and are ideal family dogs. In choosing your new best friend carefully, you are guaranteed many years ahead filled with fun and unconditional love, all the time your family is blessed with the company of a Labradoodle!

***

Understanding the short but checkered history of the Labradoodle is fundamental in any decision to bring one into your life. And if you decide to do so, it is important to avoid the many possible pitfalls as you find your perfect companion. Along with breeding issues, the price tag may seem daunting, but it is worth acknowledging that due to the arbitrary nature of Labradoodle breeding, many end up in rescue situations as they turn out to be non-hypoallergenic, too large, or have behavioral problems. Some breeders will even sell dogs that have not met the standard at a reduced price, but they will either come already neutered or with a contract to do so, to remove undesirable qualities from the gene pool. So, if you are not looking for perfection, you may be doing a valuable service in opening up your life and home to an unwanted dog, as long as you have the experience and emotional resilience to deal with any associated problems.

This book will take you through all the important considerations when deciding on a Labradoodle, and support you through all of your dog's key life stages, from training, to adolescence and adulthood, and the final farewell to a faithful companion. The years spent with your Labradoodle are sure to be full of fun for both of you so long as you take the time to learn everything necessary before bringing home your new dog.

CHAPTER 2
The Labradoodle

"Labradoodles are intelligent dogs that are typically easy to train and possess good temperaments. They are social, sensitive, and loyal. Their most unique physical characteristic is a wavy growing coat that is typically allergy friendly and non-shedding."

Rochelle Woods
Spring Creek Labradoodles

Fun, intelligent, and eager to please. Who wouldn't want a Labradoodle? But the main issue with the breed is that it is still in its early days, so consistency is lacking. Just because one Labradoodle has a certain temperament, doesn't mean the next will be the same. There are huge variations between the different geographical types of Labradoodles and the different generations, giving rise to a variety of sizes, colors, and temperaments. In this chapter, we will look at the differences seen within the breed.

Photo Courtesy of Brittany Kerr

Types

As discussed in Chapter 1, the Labradoodle originated in Australia when a Labrador and Poodle were bred to produce the original F1 (first generation) Labradoodle. However, now that the Labradoodle craze has spread across the world, there are now some distinct geographical differences.

Geographical Types

American

The US likes to claim its own version of the breed, known as the American Labradoodle. These are Labradoodles which have been bred from American Kennel Club (AKC) registered Labradors and Poodles. They are not usually named American Labradoodles if they are not an original cross.

FUN FACT

Australian Labradoodle Association of America

The mission of the Australian Labradoodle Association of America (ALAA) is "[to] protect the welfare of the Labradoodle and Australian Labradoodle breeds." The ALAA was established in 2004. The largest database of Labradoodles and Australian Labradoodles is managed by the ALAA, with information regarding more than 25,000 dogs. For information about volunteer opportunities or involvement with the ALAA, visit www.alaa-labradoodles.com

British

Similar to the US, the UK uses the names British Labradoodles, English Labradoodles, or UK Labradoodles. Again, this refers to an original cross between a registered Labrador and Poodle, and not multigenerational Labradoodles.

Australian

Although the Labradoodle is technically a cross between a Labrador and a Poodle, the Australian Labradoodle also has some other breeds infused into its bloodline. These include the English Cocker Spaniel, the American Cocker Spaniel, and the Irish Water Spaniel. As a result, the Australian Labradoodle has some genetic variation in comparison to other Labradoodles around the world.

Multigenerational Australian Labradoodles, which come from mating two other Labradoodles, are more consistent in their genetic make-up. Their coats are usually non-shedding and wavy or curly, rather than flat.

Photo Courtesy of
Donnie Padgett

Size Types

The sizes of Labradoodles can vary greatly due to the different types of Poodle mixed into the gene pool. Therefore, buying a Labradoodle does not mean you are specifically buying a small or large dog.

Standard

The standard Labradoodle is the biggest of all. The height at the wither can be 21 inches to 24 inches (53cm to 63cm) with the female being a little smaller than the male within this height range. A normal weight range is 50lbs to 65lbs (23kg to 30kg); however, the dogs can also potentially be much bigger.

Medium

The medium Labradoodle stands at 17 inches to 20 inches (43cm to 52cm) and weighs 30lbs to 45lbs (13kg to 20kg). Again, the female is usually smaller than the male.

Miniature

Miniature Labradoodles usually come from crosses with miniature Poodles, and as a result, can be very small. The height at the wither is usually 14 inches to 16 inches (35cm to 42cm) and the weight between 15lbs and 25lbs (7kg to 13kg).

"F" Numbers

If you've heard of Labradoodles, you will have certainly heard of F numbers. But all the talk of F numbers can be very confusing. F stands for filial, which derives from the Latin word filius (son). Loosely translated, it means 'relating to a son or daughter.'

What are 'F' Generations?

An F1 Labradoodle is an original cross of a Labrador with a Poodle. The original crosses can be somewhat variable, as half the genes come from a Labrador, and half from a Poodle, rather than all the genes coming from Labradoodles. An F1 Labradoodle is often a frequent shedder, although some owners of F1 Labradoodles may be lucky and have one which inherits more of the Poodle's genes when it comes to coat shedding.

Many experts believe that the F1 generation is healthier than individual pure breed generations. This is known as hybrid vigor. This is somewhat a myth, as a healthy puppy comes from two healthy parents with no genetic problems. However, those who believe in hybrid vigor believe that only the F1 generation experiences it, and the more multigenerational the Labradoodle, the more it loses this advantage.

After the F1 generation, the subsequent generations are named according to the lowest numbered parents, by adding the next number up. So, for example, an F2 Labradoodle could be two F1 Labradoodles bred together, or an F1 crossed with an F2, F3, or F4, etc. And likewise, an F3 Labradoodle is the offspring of an F2 crossed with an F2, F3, F4, or F5, etc. Once the numbers get into multiples, the type of cross is called a multigen or multigenerational cross. These are very popular, since if multigenerational Labradoodles come from a good breeder, their appearance, coat type, and temperament will be significantly more consistent and predictable. As a result, they can be expensive, reaching even tens of thousands of dollars.

Photo Courtesy of
Courtney Nadeau

What are 'B' Generations?

B generations are where the breeding becomes more complicated. The B stands for backcross. A backcross oc-

19

Photo Courtesy of Robin Norman

curs when a Labradoodle is backcrossed to one of the original breeds, a Poodle or a Labrador. Most commonly this is a Poodle, as it helps to improve the curl and quality of the coat. But as a result, the Labradoodle may end up being a higher percentage Poodle than Labrador. Later generation backcrosses may be crossed with an original breed, or a Labradoodle backcross. So, for example:

F1B (1st generation backcross) = F1 Labradoodle x Poodle

F2B (2nd generation backcross) = F1 Labradoodle x F1B Labradoodle or F2 Labradoodle x Poodle

Etc.

Age Expectancy

Labradoodles are relatively long-living dogs, with life spans averaging 12-15 years. The smaller the type, the longer they are likely to live. With that being said, there are many factors which come into play when looking at lifespan, including genetics, exercise, diet, and ill health.

Colors

One of the most common inconsistencies within the Labradoodle breed is the coat appearance. There is a large variety of potential colors and coat textures. The textures can include a straight, hair-like coat similar to that of a Labrador, a wavy fleece coat, or a curly wool coat closely resembling a Poodle. As a result, there is no guarantee what a Labradoodle puppy will turn out to look like. There are many different types of colors, and it is common for a litter to have many variations. The color of a puppy is also likely to develop or change as he reaches maturity.

Red
A red Labradoodle has a strikingly rich coat color. It's a shade of chestnut brown, with a black nose.

Apricot
An apricot Labradoodle has a rich dark gold coat, resembling the inside of a ripe apricot. The nose is always black.

Caramel
Caramel is a popular and common color. Caramel-colored Labradoodles usually have brown noses and a coat between a light yellow to a yellow with

Photo Courtesy of Marki Walls

a red hue. The difference between other Labradoodles of a similar coat color is the color of the nose.

Cream

Cream is a similar color to caramel, although just a little lighter. The main difference is that the nose pigment is black.

Blue

Blue puppies are born with a black coat with a blue pigmentation and black noses. A Labradoodle's blue coat develops over the first few years.

Silver

It is difficult to know if a puppy is going to turn silver, as the dogs usually start out black for the first few years of their lives. The color can be variable, from a light pewter to a dark charcoal. Silver Labradoodles' noses are black in color.

Chalk

As the name suggests, this color is an off-white with a black nose, similar to that of the Poodle.

Chocolate

Chocolate Labradoodles have a dark brown coat, although many become lighter with age.

Café

This color is almost beige in color, similar to the Parchment color but a bit more yellow. The nose is a brown-rose color.

Lavender

This color is a very light chocolate, which in certain lights gives off a pink or lavender color. The nose is brown-rose in color.

Black

Black Labradoodles also have black noses, and are solid in color with no other colors in the coat.

Parchment

Parchment is an unusual color similar to coffee with a generous addition of milk. It is usually a dark, dusky brown-beige, but may also be a similar color to a chocolate Labradoodle. The nose is a brown-rose color.

Mixed

Mixed colors can either be 'parti,' which is white with spots or patches of a solid color, or 'phantom,' which is a solid base color with a second color above each eye, sides of the muzzle, chest, and legs.

Hypoallergenic and Non-Shedding Coats

"Oh, and there is no such thing as a (completely) hypo-allergenic dog. Many people with allergies react less or not at all to Labradoodles, but they are not non-allergenic."

Carolyn DeBar
Doodle Around

One of the Labradoodle's common attractions is its hypoallergenic, non-shedding coat. A so-called hypoallergenic coat is one which minimally sheds and has no, or minimal, dander. However, unless the breeders have been very careful with their genetic monitoring and tested individual puppies, it is impossible to truly know whether an individual will be one which sheds its coat or has a hypoallergenic coat. However, there has now been a genetic test developed, looking for the IC gene (improper coat), which will help determine if two parents may give birth to offspring with undesirable coats.

Breed Standard

Since the Labradoodle is not yet recognized as an official breed, and is instead a 'cross' or 'designer' breed, the American Kennel Club (AKC) has not yet set an official standard for the breed. However, this does not mean your Labradoodle cannot be AKC registered. The AKC has a program called 'Canine Partners' which embraces all types of dogs. When you enroll, you will receive similar benefits to traditional registration. This includes an official certificate, eligibility to participate in events such as AKC Agility, Rally, Scent Work, Obedience, and Tracking, eligibility for AKC titles such as AKC

Canine Good Citizen, AKC Trick dog, and AKC Search and Rescue Wilderness, enrollment in AKC Reunite Lost and Found Recovery Service, a complimentary visit with an AKC Veterinary Network Veterinarian, and 30 days of pet insurance.

The British Kennel Club also allows crossbreeds to register with them on the Activity Register, to enable them to participate in events, but it has yet to publish a breed standard for the Labradoodle.

The only breed standard available is one set out by the Australian Labradoodle Association. This will be relevant to Australian Labradoodles which possess other breeds in their genetics; however, American and British Labradoodles still lack a standard to conform to.

The Australian Breed Standard for the Labradoodle (2007)

General Appearance: Must appear athletic and graceful with a compact body displaying substance with medium boning. Should not appear cloddy or heavy nor overly fine. A distinctive feature of this breed is the coat, which is non-shedding and easy to manage.

Temperament: Extremely clever, sociable, comical, joyful, energetic when free and soft and quiet when handled. The dogs should approach people in a happy friendly manner, keen and easy to train. They should display an intuition about their family members or handlers' current emotional state or needs. This ability to "know" is what has made the Australian Labradoodle an excellent dog for individuals with special needs.

Body: (to wither) as to length (from sternum to point of buttock) should appear square and compact. Deep chest and well sprung. There should be a good tuck-up. Loins should be strong and muscular.

Head: Moderately broad with well-defined eyebrows. Stop should be moderate with eyes set well apart. The head should be of moderate width; developed but without exaggeration. Foreface to appear shorter than skull. The head should be clean-cut and free from fleshy cheeks. The whole head must be in proportion to the size of the dog.

Ears: Large, expressive and slightly rounded.

Mouth: Must be a scissor bite. Upper teeth to just overlap the bottom teeth.

Nose: Should be large, of square appearance and fleshy.

Teeth: Scissor bite. Undershot or overshot bite is a major fault. Crowding teeth in miniatures is a fault.

Forequarters: Shoulders blades and upper arms to be the same length, and shoulders should be well laid back. Elbows are set close to the body. Forelegs to be straight when viewed from the front. Toeing in or out is a fault.

Hindquarters: In profile the croup is nearly flat, slight sloping of the croup is acceptable. Stifles should be moderately turned to propel forward movement, and hindquarters well-muscled for power in movement. Hock to heel should be strong and short being perpendicular to the ground. View from the rear should be parallel to each other, must not be cow-hocked.

Feet: The feet are medium size, round with well-arched toes having elastic and thick pads. Feet should not turn in or out.

Tail: The tail should follow the topline in repose or when in motion. It may be carried gaily, but should not curl completely over the back. The tip of the tail should not touch the back or curl upon itself.

Movement: The trotting gait is effortless, smooth, powerful, and co-ordinated in mature dogs. It should have a good reach in front and drive from behind for forward motion. Sound free movement and a light gait are essential.

CHAPTER 3
Getting Ready for a Labradoodle

"I always tell potential puppy families, if you like a Lab, you'll LOVE a Labradoodle. They have the friendliness and outgoingness of a Lab and the smarts of a Poodle. Most doodles think they are people and act accordingly, they love being in close contact with their family, often placing a paw on their 'person'."

Jenny Williams
Happy Go Lucky Labradoodles

It's easy to see why anyone would fall in love with the Labradoodle. Although just coming across the breed in the media can be love at first sight, if you have actually met a Labradoodle in person, maybe in the park, or owned by a friend, you are sure to have been captivated by its charm and affectionate nature. Maybe you have even found to your surprise that your friend's Labradoodle has not triggered your dog allergy, and you are now considering a dog for the first time. This book will stress many times that the Labradoodle is not necessarily hypoallergenic, but some are, so with extra special care you may find a best friend that can share your home.

Photo Courtesy of
Rose Miller

Photo Courtesy of
Laura Lord

Are You Ready?

If you have owned a dog before, you will already be aware of the adjust-ments and compromises you need to make in your life to accommodate a dog. But you will also know that the rewards of having a dog in your life tip the balance in a positive way. Having a dog around is the perfect stress-reliever, once you have gotten over the initial stress-inducing months of housebreak-ing, destruction, and training! Dogs encourage you to exercise, they show your children how to take care of others. They have even been proven to boost your immune system. But above all, the unconditional love of a dog is something that can't be measured, and puts all life's trials into perspective.

On the other hand, owning a dog means commitment. The dog needs to be exercised daily, as well as needing company for a good proportion of the day. You need to make arrangements for your dog when you go on vacation. A dog as big and shaggy as a Labradoodle will bring plenty of dirt into your home, even if you are lucky enough to find one that does not shed or smell. And the financial cost of keeping a Labradoodle will last throughout his 12-15-year lifes-pan, probably increasing with age. So all these things need to be weighed very carefully before you take the big step of bringing home a Labradoodle.

Photo Courtesy of
Ted Micucci

Costs of Keeping a Labradoodle

The first cost you will encounter when considering a Labradoodle is the actual price of the dog. It has already been noted that Labradoodles are an expensive breed, to their great disadvantage, as many breeders have seized upon a moneymaking opportunity at the expense of the welfare of their breeding stock and the puppies produced. The cost of the dog is not necessarily a reliable indicator of its quality or the ethical standards of the breeder, and the onus is on the purchaser to research both of these important points. But on average, a Labradoodle will cost between $1,000 and $2,000 to buy from a breeder, and sometimes much more.

If you have purchased a Labradoodle for a lower than average price, this may be for a number of reasons. Sometimes the breeder will not consider a particular puppy to meet the standard, and he will sell the puppy already neutered or with a contract to do so, to remove it from the breeding pool. A more inexpensive puppy might have health issues that will incur expense down the line, or he may simply be of the wrong coat texture or color. Sometimes a puppy may be returned to the breeder either because he is not hypoallergenic, or the owners have not thoroughly thought through the responsibilities of owning a dog. So you may pick up an older puppy for a lower price, but you may have to work harder to restart his training if he has missed the early months.

Sometimes puppies or older Labradoodles are advertised on websites, in which case you will have to proceed with caution, to establish the precise issues leading to the rehoming, and whether you are equipped to deal with them. Private sales and rehomings are not ideal or

Photo Courtesy of
Angela Ash

29

in the interests of the dog, as home checks are rarely carried out. It is better to support a rescue, but you will still have to pay a rehoming fee of several hundred dollars to cover costs and indicate commitment to the dog.

How well your dog has been bred is an indicator of his likely veterinary costs over the course of his lifetime. A dog that comes with known and tested parentage and health certificates is likely to lead a healthy life, whereas an unknown quantity may turn out to be a frequent visitor to the veterinary surgery, and possibly suffer from ongoing lifelong conditions affecting his quality of life. Some of these are outlined in Chapter 14. It is important to buy pet insurance from the outset, before your dog is treated for any condition that would subsequently be excluded. That way you can budget for his health care without any nasty surprises or prohibitive costs.

Ongoing health costs will include vaccinations, parasite control, dental care, and routine vet visits costing below the minimum claim threshold set by your insurance company. Food costs will vary according to your dog's size and are explained in more detail in Chapter 11.

Photo Courtesy of Dorie O'Shea

The equipment you will need to buy for your Labradoodle is largely an upfront cost, but some items such as collars, harnesses, crates, and beds may need to be replaced as your dog grows, and other items will wear out or be destroyed. The amount of money you spend on your Labradoodle's equipment is a matter of personal choice. Many owners love the shopping experience as it gives them a lot of pleasure to spoil their dog. However, as long as the items you buy are size-appropriate and well made, your dog will be just as happy whatever the cost. Those on a budget may consider buying secondhand, as long as pre-owned dog equipment has been cleaned and disinfected, and is not broken or excessively worn.

Whatever coat texture your Labradoodle has, it is sure to be thick and hairy! The hair coat is prone to shedding, so regular grooming outside will keep your house cleaner. On the other hand, the non-shedding wool coat is prone to matting, so needs special attention. The in-between, generally non-shedding fleece coat texture also needs regular grooming. Many Labradoodle owners use the services of a professional to keep their dogs' coat in good condition, and many also choose to clip their dogs during the warm summer months. Further advice on grooming is given in Chapter 12.

Photo Courtesy of Kasie Duffy

A dog is for life, and therefore it is important that you have spent plenty of time considering whether a Labradoodle is for you, and whether you have the time and finances to commit to him. If you decide to pursue getting a Labradoodle, this will be an exciting time for you. Finding a lovable Labradoodle companion can be one of the most amazing times of your life.

CHAPTER 4
Selecting a Puppy

Selecting a good Labradoodle breeder is the biggest minefield you will encounter in the acquisition of your new best friend. More so than in selecting any pedigree dog, where breeding establishments are tightly regulated by the Kennel Club. And also, more so than selecting a mixed breed, whose arbitrary breeding is compensated for by the assorted genetics canceling out inherited health conditions, and who will not be the product of a puppy farm.

The popularity and price tag of the Labradoodle has made the breed the focus of countless breeders with an eye on the money to be made, and is one reason why Wally Conron despaired of the Pandora's box he had opened. It is vital to acknowledge that even some well-known kennels with renowned Labradoodle credentials may not be all that they appear.

Photo Courtesy of
Patricia Adams

Finding a Reputable Breeder

"It is very important to make sure you are working with someone who has experience with the breed and assessing personality and temperament. Some breeders will let you choose a puppy based on looking at a picture only, or meeting the litter one time. We personally believe the most important factor in a puppy working out long term with a family, is having the right personality and temperament to fit in with that family well. An experienced breeder or rescue organization will be able to provide feedback on each puppy and guide you to the ones that will be best suited for your home, and your home best suited for them. Trust that experience."

Rochelle Woods
Spring Creek Labradoodles

In the first instance, you may be wondering how you can find a breeder of Labradoodles when the breed is not recognized by the Kennel Club. There are two options. Have you fallen for the breed because of a particular Labradoodle you have met? Maybe a friend's dog, or one you see regularly in the park? In this case, it is worth asking the owner where they purchased their dog, as you have seen for yourself that the dogs produced by this kennel have a nice nature, and to the best of their owners' knowledge, have not presented with any inherited health conditions. There is nothing to beat a firsthand recommendation. If you do not actually know a Labradoodle owner, it is worth looking at Labradoodle forums on the internet, as you will find that experiences and recommendations on internet forums are a lot franker than the glossy marketing of breeders' websites.

The other route to a well-bred Labradoodle is via the Labradoodle Club in your country. These will have a list of breeders; however, you cannot necessarily rely upon the ethics and welfare standards of these breeders, and will still need to do further research.

Above all, you should visit the breeding premises in person before committing to buy a Labradoodle puppy. You should never rely on a video produced from a breeding kennel abroad, with a view to importing a puppy to order, as you will have no reliable way of knowing the conditions in which your dog was bred or if you are inadvertently supporting a puppy farm. Your two-month-old puppy may be healthy, but do you know the condition of his mother, how she is kept, and how many litters she has been forced to breed back-to-back? And what if you need breeder support, or have to return the puppy?

It is also vitally important to visit the breeding establishment before reserving your puppy if you have a dog allergy. This is because of the common misconception that Labradoodles are hypoallergenic. Even if the breeder makes this claim for his dogs, the only way you will know for sure that you will not react is to spend the best part of a day at the kennels. A reputable breeder will not think this an unreasonable request, and should welcome the suggestion, as it helps to ensure the puppy is not returned later on due to allergy issues.

Photo Courtesy of Chrystal Sanchez

Viewing the Parents

"If choosing from a breeder the most important thing is finding a knowledgeable breeder that knows the breed and takes time to get to know you. Conscientious breeders will temperament test the puppies often and have expertise in matching you with the perfect puppy for you and not just that looks the way you want. Personality fits always trump conformation and looks and the breeder is the only one who can help peel back those layers and help make the best decision for you because they have seen the puppies daily, whereas you might only be seeing the puppy for 20 minutes and then making a decision."

Robby Gilliam
Mountain View Labradoodles

If you have visited the breeder in person, you should be able to view the mother, or the female dogs used by the kennels if none are currently pregnant or nursing. The kennels may not necessarily have the male dogs they use on the premises, as these are often owned and kept elsewhere. However, for litters that are currently expected, the breeder should be able to provide the sire's pedigrees and breeding certificates. You will also usually be able to see photographs or be able to make an appointment with the owners of the sire to visit him in person too.

Look for inbreeding when viewing pedigree charts, which is a repetition of the same names, as this can indicate a higher chance of genetic conditions being passed on. Sometimes selective inbreeding is permitted, especially in the development of a breed, and is termed line-breeding. However, this needs to be approved by the breed club, and the breeder should be able to provide documentation to this effect.

The main thing to take note of when viewing the parents is that they are kept in clean and comfortable conditions, ideally in a home environment, and not overbred. The mother should be at least 16 months of age and no older than eight years. She should have a maximum of five litters in her breeding years, with an interval of at least 10 months between each litter (variable by country). The male should be over 12 months of age, because hips and elbows cannot be tested for dysplasia before a male dog is fully grown.

Of course, with a Labradoodle, both parents may not be Labradoodles. If this is a first-generation pairing, the mother may be a Labrador Retriever, and the sire may be a Poodle. In this case, the parents should be Kennel Club certified. Sometimes a Labradoodle may also be backcrossed with a Poodle. However, if both parents are Labradoodles, their health screening certificates will be voluntary, but reputable breeders approved by the breed club will go above and beyond the basic health tests to verify that the puppies will be free of problems. You should look for a clean bill of health when it comes to hip dysplasia, elbow dysplasia, hypothyroidism, Von Willebrand disease, and Progressive Retinal Atrophy (PRA).

Be aware that a litter of Labradoodles is like Forrest Gump's box of chocolates – you never know what you're going to get! Looking at the parents is no guarantee of color, coat texture, shedding, or hypoallergenic qualities, of which any number of variations may appear in a single litter. You should, however, be able to predict temperament, health, and to some extent size. Multigenerational Labradoodles will produce more consistent puppies.

Photo Courtesy of Michelle Duggins

Choosing the Perfect Puppy

"Look for a breeder who is temperament testing at seven weeks or later. If you choose a puppy based on looks at three days or three weeks, you will know nothing about that puppy. You may want a hunting dog, and you'll end up with a couch potato. You may want a therapy dog and you'll end with a dog that can't lie still. You may be looking for a couch potato and end up with an extremely playful, high energy puppy - or vice versa. Not having a puppy with the correct temperament is one of the leading reasons dogs are turned into shelters."

Carolyn DeBar
Doodle Around

When you are viewing the breeding establishment for the first time as part of your research, there may or may not be puppies present, and if there are, they may already be reserved. You usually will have to put your name on a list for the next litter due to the popularity of Labradoodles.

So, you are at the point where you have found a reputable breeder and reserved a puppy. The breeder is unlikely to invite you to look at the puppies before they are five weeks of age, as until that time their looks and person-alities are very much in development. However, you will probably get to visit before the pups are weaned in order to select your new Labradoodle. Bear in mind that some breeders like to match their pups to applicants themselves, based on their experience of the personality traits they see coming through in the puppies, and an applicant's individual circumstances and lifestyle.

Let's assume the breeder lets you select your puppy from the litter. As previously noted, a litter of Labradoodles may all look very similar if they are multigenerational, having been bred from successive generations of Labra-doodles. Or if they are first or early generation Labradoodle puppies, the lit-ter may offer a complete assortment of colors and coat varieties. However, the coat will change as your dog matures, so if you have allergy issues, you should take advice from the breeder as to which puppy is most likely to be non-shedding and hypoallergenic. You will have a better guarantee of this with multigenerational Labradoodles.

Whenever you look at a litter of puppies, whether pedigree, hybrid, or crossbreed, the criteria are the same. The pups should be clean with no dis-charge from their eyes or ears. Their bottoms should be clean with no wet or

FUN FACT
Vice-Presidential Labradoodle

In American history, a president has never owned a Labradoodle while in office. However, Vice President Joe Biden owned a Labradoodle dog named Brother. It is unclear whether Brother ever visited Washington, D.C., with the vice president.

dry urine or feces. Their tummies should have no lumps indicative of a hernia. In the case of a male puppy, he should have two descended testicles, though these may not have yet descended at a first viewing. The puppies should be feeding well and appear vigorous, bright-eyed, and inquisitive, and they should be playing happily with their littermates.

Some people say that you should let your puppy choose you, and others claim this is bad advice, as the most dominant puppy will make the first approach, and he may turn out to be a handful as he grows! On the other hand, a shy puppy may have socialization issues. If you do not want a challenge, it is best to consider the puppies that are neither dominant nor submissive. Whether you choose a boy or a girl is a matter of preference and either will make a great pet. But if you already have a dog it is usually best to choose the opposite gender as long as your resident dog is neutered.

The puppy you choose should be happy to be handled, and if you have allergy issues, you should handle your dog as much as the breeder allows, again to test for a reaction, and revisit regularly until your collection date.

Labradoodles are often neutered at an earlier stage than other breeds to prevent unregulated breeding, and if not, they will almost always come with a contract to be neutered before the age of 18 months, often earlier.

Breeder Contracts and Guarantees

Once you have decided on a puppy, most reputable breeders will offer a contract and guarantee. These will differ between breeders, so it is important to thoroughly read the paperwork before signing. Puppy contracts are a way for breeders to outline expectations from both sides, and are a good idea to have in place.

The start of the contract should have all the factual information about the puppy that you are buying. This includes which puppy, the parents, registration details (if applicable) and microchip number (if already done). This will help you identify which is your puppy if there ends up being a dispute later on. It should also detail how much you have agreed to pay for the puppy, if you have paid a deposit, if you have already paid in full, or if you are paying in installments.

The most important part of the contract for you sets out what the breeder guarantees about the puppy. Most breeders will guarantee that the puppy is in good health at time of purchase, but some will require you to take your puppy to a veterinarian for a check-up to confirm this within 72 hours of collection. The contract will also outline any guarantees for genetic conditions. Since Labradoodles are not purebred dogs, there are no compulsory genetic tests, however many breeders will still electively test the parents for genetic diseases. As mentioned previously, this includes tests for hip dysplasia, elbow dysplasia, hypothyroidism, Von Willebrand disease, and Progressive Retinal Atrophy (PRA).

Some breeders may also put other conditions in their contracts that you must adhere to if you want that specific puppy. These might include a requirement to neuter your puppy, or a clause that you may not breed him or her without their permission. It may also state that you must get certain health tests done, such as hip and elbow scores, when he is fully grown. If the contract makes you uncomfortable, there is nothing forcing you to sign it, and you can always find another breeder. From the breeder's point of view, they are allowing one of their prize possessions to go to you, and therefore they are just wanting what is best for their puppy, as well as protecting the integrity of their breeding program.

Finally, there should be a section about conditions which can lead to returning the puppy. Most reputable breeders will accept returns under certain conditions, for example if the puppy ends up having a health issue or he doesn't settle in at your house within a certain time period.

Photo Courtesy of Donna Irizarry

Rescuing a Labradoodle

"Is the pup outgoing, friendly and happy? Those are usually good indicators of early socialization. If choosing one from a rescue, try to obtain as much history as possible to ensure a good fit. Is the pup/dog good around other pets? Children? Any known health issues? ect."

Jenny Williams
Happy Go Lucky Labradoodles

Many prospective Labradoodle owners would never think of looking for a dog of this breed in an animal shelter. This is because the Labradoodle has such a hefty price tag – how would such a dog ever find itself in a rescue? In fact, this assumption is very wrong. Labradoodles can be rehomed for many reasons, not necessarily behavioral. For example, as we have already noted, they may not turn out to be hypoallergenic and owners with allergies may not be able to cope. During the first year of the Labradoodle's life, his coat will change a couple of times. The first is probably before you even pick him up, but the next change occurs at adolescence, around eight months of age. If your hypoallergenic dog then turns out to cause an allergic reaction in a sensitive individual, it may be impossible to keep him, and at this late stage the breeder may not take him back. This is one unfortunate reason a Labradoodle may find himself in rescue.

Other reasons are less unique to Labradoodles. Dogs of all kinds may find themselves in rescue due to a change of circumstances of the owner. This may be due to work commitments, financial circumstances, health issues, or a new baby. Often a Labradoodle will be rehomed privately through local advertising, but many owners take the view that it is better to rehome their dog through a shelter that will carry out proper home checks and vetting of the new owner, and offer full rescue backup for life. They therefore forgo recouping their purchase cost in their dog's best interest.

And of course, just like any other breed, there will always be Labradoodles in rescue who have proven to be too problematic for their owners. Maybe they have not been properly trained or socialized from an early age. They will certainly need an experienced home. Or maybe they have turned out to have health problems from poor breeding. If so, they will need a home with the financial resources for their ongoing care. Or maybe they simply grew too big. In that case, they will need a bigger home. It is rare that a Labradoodle is rehomed due to aggression as this is not a common breed trait.

If you decide to adopt a Labradoodle from a rescue, you can take satisfaction in doing a really worthy thing that your dog will appreciate for the rest of his days. This route will be less costly at the outset, even though you will have to pay an adoption fee, often several hundred dollars. However, if your rescued Labradoodle has health issues that led him to be rehomed, you will not get insurance for pre-existing conditions, so the lifetime cost may be greater. Also, if he has behavioral issues requiring retraining, this may also involve the cost of an animal behaviorist. Some rescue organizations might help with this, so always ask.

Photo Courtesy of Jennifer Russell.

You will almost always be required to have a home check before you are allowed to adopt a dog from a shelter. This is to check that your personality, house, and yard are suitable for a Labradoodle, you understand the implications of dog ownership, and everyone in the household is on board with the idea.

You will also never actually "own" your dog; he will always remain in the ownership of the rescue and must be returned, not rehomed privately, if your situation changes. This is to ensure the dog never falls into the wrong hands or is sold for profit. A rescue Labradoodle will almost always be neutered before you adopt him, or you will be required to have the procedure done as soon as possible after taking the dog home. In most cases, these conditions do not make sharing your life with a rescue dog any different from a dog you had bought from a breeder; your dog will soon recognize you as his soul mate, and you will have a bond for life.

CHAPTER 5
Preparing Your Home

"Most people who have never had a puppy before are often surprised how much work goes into a new pup. Puppy proofing your home will save a lot of headaches and potential vet bills later on. Good rule of thumb: get on your hands and knees (puppy level) and look around from their perspective for anything that could be an issue: electrical cords, poisonous cleaning supplies, expensive shoes, ect."

Jenny Williams
Happy Go Lucky Labradoodles

Photo Courtesy of
Felicia Watson

Preparing Inside and Outside Spaces

"Boundaries are important so we always say having a set up where they have a small portion of the home that is easy to clean. As training and obedience is taught then they are given more and more space in the house, but when mistakes or accidents happen they lose some of their space. Run of the house or access to certain areas is a privilege and has to be earned."

Robby Gilliam
Mountain View Labradoodles

If you do not already have a resident dog, there are several things to consider before your Labradoodle comes home with you. Even if you do have a dog, you may need to make some modifications to your current setup to take into account the size of the newcomer and the stage he is at in his development and training. For example, if you are preparing to welcome a puppy, but you already have an adult dog, you may feel that your yard is secure. However, a small puppy with an urge to dig and no concept of boundaries may quickly slip under your gate or through a small crack in the fence. Even if you are adopting an adult dog, many dogs from rescue situations have a strong escape drive that your resident dog may not have, so your fences will need to be high enough to ensure he doesn't jump out.

From the outset, you need to decide which areas of your house your new dog will have access to. If you already have a dog, it will be hard to make one rule for one and one for the other, however it is not unrealistic to keep a puppy confined to certain rooms while he is being housebroken, and still in the destructive phase of his life. If your resident dog is used to sleeping upstairs but would tolerate sleeping in the same room as the puppy, this could help with separation anxiety, although the puppy should still be crated at night.

You can block off parts of your house simply by closing the doors on the rooms you wish to keep dog-free. Many dog owners opt for stairgates, either across doorways or the stairs, until a dog is trained to know where he is allowed.

The same considerations apply for whether you are going to allow your new dog on the couch. For some owners, snuggling with their dog while reading or watching TV is a meaningful part of their relationship, and there's

Photo Courtesy of
Ramona Powell

no denying it's what your dog would choose. But if he has never had that privilege, he won't miss it. The issue is that if you don't want your dog on couch, you can never allow it, even if you're not at home, to avoid confusing him. So you will need to crate your dog or keep him in the kitchen or another room where he has no access to the couch when you are out until he knows and respects the rules. These practicalities are worth bearing in mind when preparing your home for the arrival of your new dog.

Dangerous Things that Dogs Might Eat

"Check for poisonous plants in the home and yard. Make sure chemicals and cleaning supplies are out of reach. Check for loose electrical cords and move them so puppy isn't able to chew on them. Set up a private space for puppy where they can go when they are tired and don't want to be disturbed. Have exercise pens and pet gates to use and to limit the areas where puppy can go."

Rochelle Woods
Spring Creek Labradoodles

If you haven't had a dog before, it is easy to leave things around the house which your Labradoodle might eat. These can be dangerous to him. Don't assume that your puppy will only eat food lying around though. Puppies are inquisitive and may chew and swallow all manner of foreign objects which can lead to life-threatening gastrointestinal obstructions. Common inanimate objects which your puppy might swallow include socks, toys, balls, rocks, and fruit pits.

There are many other things which may also cause a problem if swallowed. They might not cause an obstruction, but they certainly could make your Labradoodle very ill. Often these are things which can be found lying around the house, so before you bring your puppy home, make sure everything is tidied away. Some of the most common poisons include over-the-counter medications, such as ibuprofen, human prescription medication, chocolate, grapes or raisins, onions, garlic, xylitol-containing chewing gum, and some plants, such as rhododendrons, tulips, and daffodils. You'll be surprised what your dog might want to eat, even if it doesn't seem very appetizing to you.

Other Household Dangers

"Watch steps, stairs, drop off decks, and spindles that they can squeeze through. Gate off carpeted areas and close doors to make the area smaller. Pick up all toys and check for cords or things that can be chewed."

Chad and Kristi Coopshaw
Riverbend Labradoodles

Other than goodies which your dog might consume, there can also be chemical hazards around the house. Some of these also have to be ingested to cause harm, but others can also be detrimental to your Labradoodle if he comes into contact with them.

Photo Courtesy of Caitlyn Hallman

Cleaning products, such as bleach, window cleaners, and bathroom cleaners, should all be put away, and the toilet seat should be left down in case your dog decides to drink from it when it has just been cleaned with bleach.

Rodenticides are also extremely hazardous, and can act as an anticoagulant to your dog's blood if ingested in any way (which includes picking up a toy which might have come into contact with it).

Strangely, dogs love the smell of antifreeze. It has a sweet smell which might entice your dog to lick or drink it. However, this can be fatal to your dog, and should be avoided at all cost.

Finally, one of the most dangerous household items of all is a battery. If your dog plays with or even swallows a battery, it can lead to severe, life-threatening mouth, throat, and stomach ulcers.

Initial Essentials

As a guide, the basic shopping list for your new dog may comprise the following items: a bed, a crate, a collar, a lead, a harness, food and water bowls, and a few indestructible toys such as an antler, a Kong®, and a Nylabone®. These items do not need to be new, as there is a strong chance that your puppy may destroy them as he begins to teethe. However, if they are secondhand, they certainly should be in good condition, thoroughly disinfected, and have no loose or fraying parts.

You should also buy a bag of the brand of dog food which the breeder is currently feeding your puppy, so that you can slowly transition him over to the food you wish for him to eat, instead of making a sudden change when you bring him home.

Buying a Dog Bed

When it comes to choosing a bed, people often think the bigger the better. But the reality is, your puppy is likely to feel most secure in a bed a little bigger than his body. That way, he can feel the sides of it close to him, like he would have felt his littermates when they curled up together. This means you will probably have to replace the bed several times as he grows.

There are several different types of bed you can buy. Popular types include hard shell bases with soft inner cushions, flat stuffed beds, or beds with soft sides. There is no right or wrong type. When choosing a bed, apart from size, there are a few things to consider. Firstly, the thickness. If you have an older Labradoodle, a thicker bed might be better than a thinner bed, as Labradoodles are prone to joint dysplasia and arthritis. A thicker bed will help support these joints. Next, you will want to think about the inner material. The options are usually foam, stuffing, or beads. This might be particularly important to think about if you have a puppy, as puppies like to shred their beds when they are teething; beads will certainly make a mess! Finally, the last thing to consider is the outer cover. It should be comfortable, yet tough and water resistant. It should also be removeable so that you can wash it if it becomes dirty.

Buying a Crate

""If crate training, don't make the mistake of giving your puppy a huge crate to move around in. If they can pee in one space and lay in another they will, but are far less likely to if they have to lay in their mess."

Robby Gilliam
Mountain View Labradoodles

Buying a crate for your puppy is essential if you want to crate train your Labradoodle. Dogs are den animals in the wild, and therefore there are many emotional benefits for your dog. Crate training will be addressed in Chapter 8, but first you must buy the crate. There are four different types of crate you can choose from. Wire crates can collapse, which makes them easy for transport and storage. They have excellent airflow if you live in a warm climate. Plastic crates are the sturdiest and can be cleaned easily. They are the most ideal type for airline travel. Soft-sided crates are lightweight and flexible. They make comfortable dens for your dog, however if you have a dog which chews, they are the most destructible. Finally, there are wooden

Photo Courtesy of
Anna Pruett

Photo Courtesy of
Lilla Mizser

crates. These are not as common as the others as they don't have any supe-rior features, apart from the fact that they are the most stylish.

When you are deciding what size crate to buy, you should buy one which has enough space for your dog to stand up, turn around, stretch, and lie down without touching the sides. If it is bigger than that, your dog may choose to sleep on the one side and use the other as a toilet. If you want to purchase a crate for your dog to grow into, you should look into one that has dividers, so that you can adjust the size. Alternatively, you can place a cardboard box on one side of the crate to make it smaller.

Once you've purchased your puppy a crate, you will want to make it homey. Place a blanket or a bed in there, with some toys. You will want to make him feel like it is his safe space. It is best to place it somewhere in the house that is out of the way, but ventilation is important, so placing it in a corner where there is no free flow of air might make your dog feel warm in it.

CHAPTER 6
Bringing Them Home

"Take some time off to bond and work one on one with your new puppy. If you are not going to be able to watch and pay attention to your puppy, have a safe space (with access to a potty area if puppy will be alone for hours) for your puppy. Have lots of chew toys in easy reach wherever you may be in your home--when the puppy gets nippy hand it a chew toy. It is not enough to tell a puppy 'no, don't bite people', you must also tell it what it CAN bite. I highly recommend having a couple crates--a fairly large one in the room you spend the most time within, and a smaller one in your room at night. Or you can have one you move from room to room. Labradoodles are extremely social dogs and do NOT do well if left alone all night."

Carolyn DeBar
Doodle Around

Photo Courtesy of
Laurie Page

Photo Courtesy of
Dorie O'Shea

The Importance of Having a Plan

"Be prepared to be impressed. Every day of a dog's life, especially a puppy, is important. A puppy needs purposeful attention to mold them up to what you want as an adult. Expose them to as much as you can while keeping them safe. They are depending on you."

Jenny Walters
Blessings Labradoodles

Finally, the day has arrived to bring your Labradoodle puppy home! When you set out for the kennels, be sure to bring a crate in the car as well as lots of old towels. Bring your new puppy's collar and leash, and if you have to travel more than two hours or the weather is hot, bring water and a bowl. If you have to stop on the return journey for your puppy to take a comfort break, be sure to do so in a confined area in case he should slip his new collar. A rope slip lead is useful in addition to the collar and lead with a brand new dog, but sensible vigilance is key. Also, until your pup-

Photo Courtesy of
Melissa Rodriguez

py has completed his first course of vaccinations it is advisable not to stop where a lot of other dogs have been exercised.

When you arrive home with your puppy, it is obviously a very exciting time. However, for your new dog it may be rather overwhelming. Not only is he in a strange place with people he does not know, but he is away from his mother and his littermates, probably for the first time. You should keep introductions quiet and low key, allowing your new puppy to explore his new surroundings at his own pace. Be sure he knows where to find the water bowl, but other than that, allow him to make himself at home without too much interference. He is sure to be tired, and after the initial excitement has subsided, he will be ready for a long sleep!

The First Night Home

"A lot of new puppy owners don't realize that during the first 48 hour adjustment phase the puppy often will refuse to eat because of the transition. It is important not offer super enticing treats and alter their food from what you plan to provide long-term because they will come to expect this and refuse to eat their normal diet."

Jeana Bigelow
Blue Ridge Labradoodles

The first night home will be a restless one for all members of the family. It will be the first night away from his mother and littermates, and he will be feeling lonely. As a result, he will probably whine for a large portion of the night. There are several ways which you can help settle him at night though.

Firstly, ensure he sleeps in a crate. This will be like a den for him. But what is most important about the crate is that it is not too big for him. You can also make it cozy with stuffed toys and bedding. Stuffed toys are nice for puppies to snuggle up next to, as they provide comfort and warmth. You can even bring

Photo Courtesy of
Laura Lord

Photo Courtesy of Diane Walsh

the stuffed toy with you when you first meet the litter, and then bring it home with your puppy when you collect him, so that he has a toy which smells of his littermates. When choosing a stuffed toy, be sure it is specifically made for dogs, as it will be tougher to withstand chewing, and will not have choking hazards such as hard eyeballs or synthetic hair, which may be found on children's toys.

When he whines, under no circumstances should you pick him out of his crate and take him to bed with you. This is an undesirable habit which is difficult to break. You may have to take him out of his crate to relieve himself in the yard during the night, but afterwards you should put him straight back in his crate. You shouldn't give him any treats or play with him at this stage, as he needs to learn it is nighttime and therefore he doesn't get any extra attention.

With persistence, your puppy will very quickly learn to settle at night.

"A week or two of disrupted sleep is very common when you bring a new puppy home. Many families are not prepared for the initial crate training adjustment for puppy, or for having to take puppy out in the middle of the night for a potty break. This usually only lasts a week or two, but it is very common for us to receive emails from tired families who need a little encouragement to continue working through the adjustment process."

Rochelle Woods -
Spring Creek Labradoodles

Introducing to Other Pets

"For other pets inside the home, start off with the pup in their crate, where they feel safe and expose them to his or her new furry family members slowly. When it's clear everybody is going to get along, try letting the pup out to investigate on his or her own. This would be a good time to pass out treats to everybody. Keep it positive."

Jenny Williams
Happy Go Lucky Labradoodles

If you already have a dog, it is a mistake to walk through the front door with your new puppy and expect your resident dog to be impressed! In the weeks leading up to bringing your Labradoodle home, it is sensible to invite friends' dogs over to your house, so that your dog gets used to sharing his territory. This will ease the tension of the first introduction. However, it is best for your resident dog and the new puppy to meet outside in a secure backyard, where they have lots of space and can take things at their own pace. The other strategy is to take the resident dog outside of the house while the new puppy makes himself at home, and then bring the resident dog inside to find the newcomer already on the premises, rather than bringing the new dog through the door to meet the dog in residence.

If you have cats, you should take care to protect the puppy from a well-aimed swipe of a claw, as cats are adept at looking after themselves, and it is your dog that may come off worse. If you are bringing an adult Labradoodle into your home, you should check first if he tolerates cats, as it can be more challenging to change the attitude of an older dog than to bring a puppy up in the company of an established household cat. Dog rescue organizations often cat-test their dogs in foster homes prior to rehoming.

Care should always be taken with small pets such as rabbits, guinea pigs, rodents, and chickens when a dog is around. However, most Labradoodles can be socialized with household pets, and will learn that if they are important to you, they should be left alone.

Photo Courtesy of
Gwen Benedict

Introducing to Children

"Puppies explore their world with their mouths, just like babies so be very diligent in keeping them safe. If they try to bite fingers and toes give them a firm NO and then tap their nose with your finger."

Dixie Springer
Springville Labradoodles

Labradoodles make superb family pets. That said, all children, whatever their age, should be taught from the outset how to behave around dogs, as however even-tempered the Labradoodle may be, it is always possible to unfairly push a dog to the limits of its tolerance.

Before you bring your new dog home, you should give your child or children plenty of opportunity to be around friends' well-natured dogs. Teach them how to approach a dog calmly from the side so the dog can see them, and to gently stroke the dog on the back of the neck to say hello. Then if the dog is accepting, they can gently stroke its back and the top of the head and talk to it softly. Teach them never to startle a dog, pull its ears or tail, poke its eyes, or ride it like a pony. And be sure that your child knows never to pet a dog when it is eating or sleeping. Older children can be taught to recognize a dog's body language. For example, when a dog draws its lips back it is telling you to back off, and giving a warning sign that it may bite. And when a dog goes rigid, it is also not enjoying the attention. But a relaxed dog with bright eyes, an open mouth, and a waggy tail is up for a game – as long as it doesn't get too rough!

Growing up with a dog around is the best education a child can receive in caregiving and respect. You should involve your child as far as possible in your dog's daily needs, feeding, walking, and trips to the vet. This way, not only will your child learn valuable lessons that aren't taught in school, but your dog will learn to respect the child as being above himself in the pecking order, discouraging him from challenging the hierarchy and dominating the child.

Photo Courtesy of
Kelly Lindloff

The First Vet Visit

You should always take your puppy to the vet within the first few days of bringing him home. It helps you not only to get to know your vet, but also check that the puppy is healthy. If he isn't, then you may be able to return him to the breeder.

A puppy check usually doesn't include the first vaccines; however, if the breeder hasn't already got these done for you, then you may wish to have the first injection while you are there. Vaccinations are covered in more detail in Chapter 13. A puppy check will involve your vet firstly checking in the mouth. He will be looking for abnormalities such as poorly erupted deciduous teeth, an undershot or overshot jaw, or a cleft palate. Next he will check the eyes for their eyelid conformation. Entropion (eyelids turning in) or ectropion (eyelids turning out) can cause eye problems and sore eyes as your dog grows up. After the eyes, he will check the heart for any murmurs, which might suggest developmental defects. He will also feel the gut, to feel if they are inflamed, as puppies are prone to picking up parasites at this age. And finally, he will check for an umbilical hernia.

After the vet visit, if there are any issues, you can address this with the breeder. Some breeders will happily accept a return of the puppy, and some might agree to contribute to a portion of the vet costs.

Puppy Classes

"Labradoodles are very easy to train. It's usually the owners that need training, so a puppy class helps the new owner learn how to communicate with their new pup. The time you put in up front really pays off."

Sheila Flores
Oregon Labradoodles

Puppy classes are sometimes run by your local vet practice, and if they aren't, then your vet will be able to recommend a local one which is reputable. Attending puppy classes is a good idea, as these are a brilliant starting point for socializing your puppy. Many behavior problems are rooted in poor socialization.

Puppy classes usually start with free-play, allowing puppies to interact with each other. For the quieter puppies, a good facilitator will arrange the class so that suitable puppies can play together in small groups, to allow puppies to build up confidence. After a few sessions of playing, some basic commands might be introduced, such as sit, stay, and walking on a leash. However, some puppy classes may leave the commands for when your puppy graduates to basic training classes.

Separation Anxiety

Separation anxiety is a common Poodle breed trait, whereas the more relaxed Labrador Retriever is less commonly affected, even though both breeds love their humans unconditionally, and want to be with them day and night.

If you are bringing home a puppy, it is highly likely that he will suffer separation anxiety in the early weeks, as he is not used to being alone. He has only ever known the company of his littermates, and never been far from his breeder. You are now the parent on which he has imprinted his dependence, and your puppy may be stressed if you leave the room or want him to sleep on his own downstairs at night.

With regard to his sleeping arrangements, crate training your puppy is highly recommended, as not only will he be safely contained when you are not there, but he will soon see his crate as his safe den, and relax when he is in it. This will help with separation anxiety at night, especially if he has had a good evening walk or play, and is physically and mentally tired.

The crate is also an asset when you need to go out and leave your dog home alone, as you will know he is not destroying the house and is in a safe space where he feels relaxed. If your dog is upset when you leave him, you will need to build up the time he is left by gradual increments. Never make a big fuss when you leave, nor when you return, or your dog will think there really was something to worry about. Just put him quietly in his crate with a treat, and when you return, let him out without a fuss, and wait until he is quiet and has settled down, then reward him with some attention and a biscuit.

In the early stages, just leave your dog for a minute, but build this up gradually. However never leave your dog for more than 4 hours without making arrangements for him to be let out, if you cannot get back yourself within this time frame.

Many owners find a dog-cam useful, as you can observe your dog's behavior when you are not in the room. You may be pleasantly surprised to see that the whining soon stops, and your dog settles down for a peaceful sleep until he hears you return. On the other hand, if you see your dog remains stressed, you may need to take things more slowly, and go back to leaving him only for short periods.

Some owners find that leaving the radio or television on helps with separation anxiety, as it distracts the dog, makes him feel someone is there, and masks noises from outside.

Apart from gradually building up the time spent away from your anxious dog, another thing that may help with separation anxiety is a canine companion. Labradoodles are sociable and usually enjoy the company of other dogs, so an easygoing friend may give your Labradoodle a sense of security and a behavior model. He will feel less alone when you are not there. However, two dogs with separation anxiety will not be good company for each other, but will make their anxieties worse, so do choose his friend carefully. It is best to raise two puppies together, as then they will grow up knowing the hierarchy in the household; however, if you only introduce the second dog later in life, do so in a sensitive manner to your existing dog, allowing him time out and away from the new addition. This way they can slowly start to figure out their positions in the household, without adding additional stress.

With a dog suffering extreme separation anxiety, however, this will not be alleviated by the presence of another dog, as the dog is stressed at being separated from human company. If you have purchased a puppy, you are less likely to find yourself in this situation, as you are in command of his training and socialization from the outset, to create a settled and confident dog. However, if you have adopted an older Labradoodle from a shelter, you should have been made aware by the rescue organization if he has separation anxiety issues. It is quite often the main reason why a dog finds itself in rescue, especially if the dog's previous family had work commitments and could not be around during the day. Therefore, any reputable rescue will be keen to identify separation anxiety in dogs, and will only rehome them with appropriate families who can provide the necessary attention.

CHAPTER 7
Personality

"These dogs are super personable and love to communicate what they are feeling. They will let you know if they are happy, sad, discontent, etc. It is very important to not overdo indulgence with this breed because they will learn how to get their way even in the negative habits."

Jeana Bigelow
Blue Ridge Labradoodles

Although Labradoodles come in all shapes, sizes, and colors, the one thing that should be relatively consistent is their larger than life personality! In fact, this is the main draw of the breed, and more reliable than the promise of a non-shedding hypoallergenic coat.

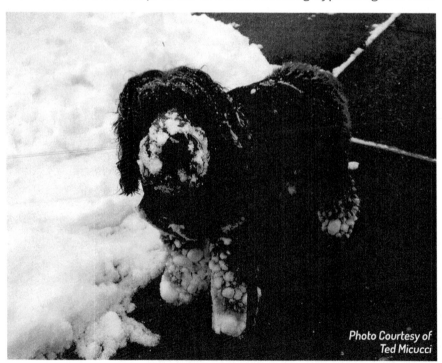

Photo Courtesy of Ted Micucci

Photo Courtesy of Lilla Mizser

Temperament

"Their personalities are what set the Labradoodle apart. They are fun and playful, yet light and easy going."

Jenny Walters
Blessings Labradoodles

Just as with any hybrid mix, the Labradoodle is a product of the parents' breed characteristics and temperaments. Therefore, with so much variety in the Labradoodle mix across the globe, from straight Labrador/ Poodle crossbreeds, to multigenerational Labradoodles, and the Australian Labradoodle that has other breeds in the mix, you might expect a whole range of temperaments. However, every reputable breeder of Labradoodles is aiming for the same goal, and that is an intelligent, affectionate family dog.

First generation Labradoodles (F1), bred from a Labrador Retriever and a Poodle, are the most likely to show a diversity in temperament, according to the proportion of each breed they inherit. However, the Labrador and the Poodle share many common characteristics that should be passed on, and these include intelligence, a sense of fun, trainability, plenty of energy, and a loving nature. Differences of temperament that can emerge in the litter may reflect the Poodle's natural reserve with strangers, quieter nature, stubbornness, or sensitivity. Early socialization of the Labradoodle will help build your dog's confidence if he has not inherited the naturally gregarious temperament of the Labrador Retriever!

The advantage of a first-generation pairing is that both pedigree breeds should be Kennel Club registered, and very carefully selected for temperament along with the usual health screening. So the parents should have more tightly documented personality credentials.

However, multigenerational Labradoodles will have more predictable temperaments, because of the fact that both parents are of the same breed. Parent breeding stock is almost always selected on the basis of excellent temperament, so unless any other breed has been injected into the mix to present a rogue gene, you should have some guarantee that your multigen Labradoodle puppy will be a typical lovable livewire. However, there is no substitute for meeting your puppy in person, and making that connection before you take him home.

Photo Courtesy of Blair Brainard

Photo Courtesy of Erin Bock

Bear in mind that your Labradoodle will usually be a boisterous dog, and if he is the product of a Standard Poodle rather than a miniature, he will grow to be large in size. So you will need to consider whether you and the family can cope with a large and lively dog, and teach him some manners at an early stage, to prevent his natural exuberance causing injury to others as he grows. Bringing an adult Labradoodle with no training into a household with very young children, or elderly people, is probably not a good idea.

Photo Courtesy of
Donna Hinde

Playing and Toys

"After the puppy has had all of its puppy shots, you can take him places for socialization. Join Facebook groups to meet other people that have Labradoodles and Goldendoodles. Most of them organize doodle romps. It's fun to go and meet other doodles, possibly including some from your breeder. Also, your dog can socialize with your friends' dogs."

Dixie Moore
Dixie's Doodles

The Labradoodle is a very playful dog by nature, and will provide endless amusement and engagement for all the family. Playing is also a perfect way to provide extra exercise and mental stimulation, as the breed requires plenty of physical activity, and has a low boredom threshold.

Labradoodles, however, can be destructive, especially at the puppy stage while they are teething, so any toys that you give your dog should be as indestructible as possible, and inspected for damage every day. A starter kit for your Labradoodle may include a Nylabone®, which is a nylon bone-shaped chew that will not splinter or break, and a Kong®, which is a hollow rubber cone that can be chewed or filled with treats for your dog to enjoy extracting. You can use a portion of your dog's regular food for this, or fill the Kong® with a soft treat such as pâté or peanut butter. You should check the label to ensure that the peanut butter you are using does not contain xylitol, an artificial sweetener that is toxic to dogs.

Deer antlers are also excellent chews for Labradoodles as they do not splinter. For this reason, they are safer than bones, and cooked bones especially should never be given. Your teething puppy needs to chew to soothe discomfort, and unless you give him appropriate toys, he will set to work on your slippers or furniture. Avoid rawhide chews, which usually contain chemicals and can cause obstructions when swallowed.

Your Labradoodle is likely to go crazy for a ball! There are, however, some important points to bear in mind. Firstly, your puppy should not play fetch at high speed, as his young bones and developing joints

67

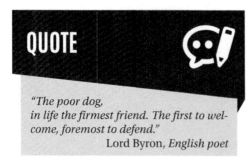

are not ready for sharp turns and stresses. Even adult dogs need moderation in games of fetch, and ball slingers can do a lot of harm if used excessively. Secondly, choose your ball carefully. Tennis balls are not recommended, as they can break in half and lodge in a dog's airway or stomach. They also have a fiber coating that is not digestible. Even some solid tennis-type balls marketed at dogs have this coating, which dogs love to chew off if left unsupervised. A solid rubber ball is best. Your dog may love to bury this in the yard, so you might choose to allow him a special digging area to save turning your whole yard into the surface of the moon. Also, your adult Labradoodle may enjoy retrieving a deflated football, which he can grip in his mouth, and is too large to choke on.

Other retrieve toys include a rubber ring, a rubber stick, or a Frisbee. Those that float in water can be fun for your water-magnet Labradoodle. Dogs should never be allowed to retrieve or chew natural sticks as these frequently lodge in the throat where they may pierce the soft tissues. Any vet will testify to the dangers of stick injuries.

Rope toys are popular with dog owners, but they should be checked daily for fraying, and discarded if they have loose fibers.

Most dogs enjoy a game of tug-of-war with a rope toy, rubber ring, or rubber figure-8 toy. However, some trainers advise caution with these games. This is because if the dog is constantly allowed to win, he may develop a feeling of dominance. In particular, children may let the dog win because the dog is stronger, and dogs readily dominate children in the family hierarchy. This is worth bearing in mind if you see any evidence of dominant behavior in your Labradoodle.

Snuffle mats are a new kind of toy to occupy your Labradoodle's busy mind. These are mats made of deep pile fleece strips, in which you can hide a portion of your dog's kibble, or small treats. Wash them regularly as the textile fibers will harbor bacteria. If your Labradoodle wolfs his food, he may also be offered the challenge of a greedy-feeder, which is a plastic plate containing molded projections that your dog must navigate with his tongue to extract his dinner.

There are other opportunities for your dog to indulge his playful nature that do not include toys. The most obvious is playing with other dogs. If you do not have a playmate for him at home, then puppy classes are a great way to start. A well socialized Labradoodle will then be able to enjoy the dog park that much more. Do not let your dog approach another dog that is on a leash, and watch out for defensive body language in the other dog, such as rigidity or the gums being drawn back. Remember the three-second rule. When your dog greets another dog and they start to sniff each other, if either shows a defensive attitude for three seconds, it is time to walk your dog away before a confrontation occurs.

Intelligent, active dogs such as Labradoodles may also enjoy agility and flyball once they are fully grown. More information on these activities is given in Chapter 9.

CHAPTER 8
Training

"Labradoodles are extremely smart and need a good foundation of manners early on. Their energy, if not channeled in a positive way, can lead to bad behavior. Oftentimes, especially with the popularity of the Labradoodle, a new owner has an "idea" of this perfect dog that will automatically happen. This is not the reality. Yes, Labradoodles are amazing dogs with very desirable traits; however, good dogs are made, not just born. It will take work, consistency, and a lot of patience to make any dog an obedient, well-behaved part of your family."

Jenny Williams
Happy Go Lucky Labradoodles

Labradoodles are bred to be human companions, and by nature there is nothing they want more than to share their life with you. However, to achieve a happy partnership, they will need to apply their innate intelligence to learning a few rules. The good news is, Labradoodles are very trainable with consistent and firm reward-based training. The principle of this is that rather than punish negative behaviors, your dog is encouraged to produce a desired behavior, and is then rewarded for doing so. This gives him a great incentive to please you, and strengthens your bond.

Being consistent and firm is particularly important with your Labradoodle because although he is smart, his Poodle genes may make him stubborn. He may also grow to be a large, boisterous dog, so it is especially important that he does not become a handful when he gets older.

Whether you are starting with a puppy, or retraining a rescue dog, local dog training classes are highly recommended. And because your training methods should be consistent, the tips given in this chapter are just a suggestion, and you should stick with what you are being taught in your classes – unless after giving it a fair chance, things still aren't working for you. Most classes teach positive reinforcement, using small treat rewards, and often a clicker too. Clickers work particularly well with Labradoodles, as they are a clear and consistent signal that he has done what has been asked of him.

Photo Courtesy of Debbie Allsopp

You may be given a clicker in your first class. If not, you can buy them at the pet store or online.

If you are new to dog training and feel out of your depth, you should never feel bad about calling in a professional to help you. In most cases this will nip negative behavior in the bud. Also, it is reassuring to have support when training your dog, as it should be fun for both of you, rather than a stressful experience.

Photo Courtesy of
Betsy Glennon

Types of Training

There are four types of training which a dog trainer might adopt. Different types of training will suit each individual dog, but generally rewarding, kind but firm training will establish a loving bond, where your dog still respects you as master.

Positive Reinforcement

"They are very easy to train, but prefer positive reinforcement and clicker training. They like to think that the training was their idea, and not be forced. They are motivated by fun, attention, and sometimes a yummy treat."

Chad and Kristi Coopshaw
Riverbend Labradoodles

Positive reinforcement is when the dog's action leads to a reward. An example is when your dog sits, you feed him a treat. This is a popular way of training for most trainers. As mentioned already, some trainers use a clicker as a positive reward. This is when if your dog does something good, the clicker is clicked, and then a treat is given. Soon, your dog will associate the click with a reward. This allows an instant, non-distracting, consistent reward to be given every time.

Positive Punishment

Positive punishment is when the action of the dog makes something bad happen. For example, the dog gets shouted at for bad behavior. It is not common that reward-based trainers will use positive punishment.

Negative Reinforcement

Negative reinforcement is when the action of the dog causes something bad to go away. For example, when a dog is lying down, but the trainer wants them to stand, so they place pressure on the neck through pulling on the leash. When the dog stands up, the leash goes slack, taking away the uncomfortable pressure.

Negative Punishment

Negative punishment is when the behavior of the dog causes a good thing to go away. A classic example is when a dog jumps up, and the person turns their back on them, causing their attention to go away.

Importance of Socialization

"One thing I suggest is meeting the new pets outside the home, so there isn't any sort of 'possession' aggressiveness. If you are bringing a new puppy into your home, I recommend rubbing a bully stick all over the new puppy before giving it to the resident dogs. The entire time they are enjoying their treat, they smell the puppy and by the time they are done, hopefully the puppy is just part of the family."

Carolyn DeBar
Doodle Around

Photo Courtesy of Katherine Horn

Your breeder will have started the socialization process before you even collected your new puppy, as the earlier a dog has positive encounters with other dogs and humans, the less likely he is to be reactive later on. But these early weeks are just the start, and the most important part of your Labradoodle's training when you get him home is to continue his socialization.

FUN FACT
Celebrity Labradoodle ☺

Many celebrities have owned Labradoodles over the years. Neil Young, singer-songwriter, owned a Labradoodle named Carl. Carl was featured in the music video for "Johnny Magic." Carl passed away in 2010. "That ol' hound dog sure meant a lot to me," said Young.

Puppy classes are ideal for this, because they give your dog a chance to mix with other pups at the same life stage, and puppies have a language of their own that your dog will have missed since he was separated from his littermates. Your puppy can start classes and mingle with other dogs as soon as he has had his first vaccinations. Puppy classes often progress to training classes after a few weeks, so your Labradoodle may graduate with his new friends and go through school together!

If you have adopted an older dog that is nervous or reactive, you may decide that classes are too stressful for him, and you need to socialize him on a one-to-one basis with other dogs. This is usually best on neutral ground, by going for a quiet walk with a friend that has a calm and friendly dog. From here you can build up his circle of trusted canine companions, and start to meet on his home territory and on his friends' territories. Each small step will gradually socialize your nervous dog until he feels more comfortable around dogs that he is meeting for the first time.

The worst setback that can happen during the socialization process is for an encounter to go wrong. It is your job to recognize the body language of your dog and the dog he is meeting, as there will usually be signs that a confrontation is going to occur. This begins with rigidity and a drawing back of the gums. And if the dogs stare each other out for more than three seconds, this is the time to walk away.

Keeping your dog's experiences positive, even though it may involve hypervigilance on your part, will ensure he grows up to love the company of his own kind, almost as much as he loves you!

Basic Commands

"They are one of the easiest breeds we have found to train if you are matched with the right personality. This is why finding a breeder that temperament tests and will match you with the perfect fit for you is so important. If their personality matches up the training is a breeze because they fit right into your life and lifestyle."

Robby Gilliam
Mountain View Labradoodles

Teaching your dog basic commands is a great way of bonding with your Labradoodle, as well as keeping him safe and under control. Before attempting to teach any command, you need your Labradoodle's complete attention. If he is a typical food-motivated Labradoodle, he will already be very focused on the treats in your pocket. However, if he has lots of distractions, such as other puppies in the class, he may be feeling very conflicted. It is important to keep up the training in the quiet of your own home or yard to consolidate your successes.

Sit

Crouch or sit down, and place your dog facing you. Let him be aware of the treat in your closed hand and tell him to "Look at me." When you have his full attention, give him the treat, or click and treat if you are using the clicker. This is the first step with any command.

Now that your dog knows there are treats up for grabs, he is ready to learn. It is important that you do not use any command word in the early stages before your dog knows what it means. You will only use the word "Sit" at the point he is sitting, so he associates the word with the action. You need to produce a sit without forcing your dog into position.

To do this, with your dog's attention on you, put your hand containing the treat to the dog's nose, then raise it up and over the dog's head. As his head follows the treat up, his hind quarters will instinctively lower. At this point, use the word "Sit." As soon as his butt hits the floor, you can give him a treat, or click and treat.

Labradoodles, especially puppies, can be energetic and wriggly, so if the process to create a sit seems to take a long time, you may find placing a hand on his bottom, without pushing, will encourage him into position.

Don't prolong your training sessions past his concentration span, which may be very short, and always aim to end on a positive note.

Lie Down

Once your Labradoodle has mastered the Sit, along with the promise of a reward, he is ready to learn 'Lie down.' Some people just use the word 'Down' for this, as long as 'Down' is not used when your dog jumps up, when 'Off' should be used instead.

With your dog in the Sit, remain in position facing him, and bring a treat to his nose, then lower it to the floor. Keep it in your hand as your dog's nose follows it, then bring it along the floor toward you. At this point, your dog will creep his front legs along the floor as he lowers his shoulders. This automatically creates the Lie Down position, so as his elbows hit the floor, you can use the words "Lie down" and give him the treat.

Quite often, as the dog lowers his front legs, his hind quarters will go back up, which isn't what you want. If your Labradoodle does this, a trick you can use is to draw the treat further toward you, with your free arm across his back like a limbo pole. In shuffling forward, he has to lower his hind quarters under your arm.

Lie Down is a bit more challenging than Sit, so be patient; it is a very worthwhile command to master, and gives you control over your dog in situations where he might make a nuisance of himself.

Stay

Stay is a potentially life-saving command. It overrides your Labradoodle's instinct to follow you or do his own thing, and it asks an exuberant, energetic dog to remain quietly in one place. You can credit your dog with a high level of obedience when he masters the command Stay.

To start with, you may need a helper to hold your dog as you move away, as his instinct will be to follow you until he understands the command. With your dog in the Sit or Lie Down position, and his attention fully focused on you, turn your outstretched palm to the dog and take a step backward. Use the word "Stay" as your helper is ensuring he is staying, then step forward and treat your dog.

Repeat the exercise until you are taking several steps back. When your dog seems to have gotten the idea and is no longer straining to follow you, your helper can release his collar, but still stay by his side. From here, the helper can let go, and your dog can remain in the Stay on his own. When your dog is really reliable at staying, you can turn your back on him as you walk away. Finally, you can practice the Stay outdoors with all the added distractions.

Some trainers like to teach the "Free" command in conjunction with the Stay. This releases your dog from the Stay on your terms. If you choose to do this, when you return to your dog, bring the treat to his nose and then away with a sweep of your arm, giving it to him as he gets up to follow your hand, and say "Free." Then let your dog stretch his legs before the next exercise.

Walking on a Leash

Teaching your Labradoodle how to walk nicely on a leash is particularly important if he has been crossed with a Standard Poodle, because he will grow into a large and strong adult dog. Even if he has been bred as a miniature, pulling on the leash will do him no favors, as it stresses his bones and muscles. It can also cause injury to his handler. So walking on a loose leash should be taught from the outset.

Although harnesses are a good idea, as they divert stresses away from the delicate neck area, teaching a dog to walk on a short leash is normally done initially off a collar, so that he feels the difference between a contact and a loose leash. You should never use a choke chain; these can cause serious damage.

To begin with, your Labradoodle puppy may think the leash is a toy, and he may constantly try to bite it. You need to distract him from the leash, and focus his attention on you.

With the leash in your right hand and treats in your left, position the dog on your left-hand side, gain his attention by showing him the treat, and take a few steps forward. To begin with, your dog may jump around all over the place – after all, he is a Labradoodle! But this will not bring him a reward. Sooner or later, your dog will walk a few paces to the treat. Don't ask for any more than that, but reward this good start with a treat and praise. Now he knows what you want. Get his attention again and repeat the exercise. Increase the number of steps before giving the treat. If your dog rushes ahead, stop. Wait for him to settle, then move forward again.

If you have started this training in an indoor space, such as at training classes, you may find your puppy seems to have the idea, but once you get outside, he might be a hooligan. With the promise of outdoor smells and a proper walk, your dog is likely to be keen to drag you to where he wants to go. However, it is important to understand that this is training on your terms, not recreation on his, and an hour-long romp in the countryside is not on today's agenda. In fact, you may not cover much ground at all to start with, as every time your dog pulls on the leash, you need to stop, only moving forward when the leash is loose again. Remember to feed treats to your dog every time he is walking nicely and tell him he is a good boy.

You will not always have to feed your dog treats as a reward for walking on a loose leash, but even when he has the behavior ingrained in him, you should still always praise him for walking nicely. This will go a long way to building his confidence and his desire to please you.

Crate Training

"Labradoodles can be a bit stubborn to crate train since their goal in life is to be with their family!"

Carol Finch
Acme Creek Kennels

Crate training can take a bit of time and patience, but if done successfully, it can be very useful in many situations. Crates can be used for sleeping in, traveling in, restricting access to the house, giving your dog some time out when you have visitors over, and for providing him with a safe space for him to go if he is anxious.

As previously discussed, don't make the mistake of buying a large crate for your dog to grow into, because if your dog has enough room to sleep in one corner and soil another, crate training will be counterproductive. A smaller crate, where your dog still has enough room to stand, turn and lie down, is actually comforting to your dog, and feels more like a den. A crate is not a prison, but somewhere your dog can feel relaxed and safe if he is used to it from a puppy. Keeping the door open when you are around, and putting inside soft bedding, toys and treats helps with acceptance.

The first step is to introduce your dog to the crate. You should initially put the crate somewhere that you spend a lot of time. The door should be securely fastened open, so it can't accidentally close or bash your dog. You should encourage your dog to explore the crate and go in by placing some small treats or his favorite toy just inside the door. He may instantly go in, or it may take a few days to build up his confidence. Either way is fine.

After your dog happily goes in and out the crate, then next step is to start feeding him in it. This gives him a positive association with the crate. After a few times, you can close the door while he eats the meal, but immediately open it afterward. With each successive meal, you can keep it closed for a few minutes longer after the meal, until he's been in there for up to 10 minutes. If he starts whining, you may have increased the time too quickly, and therefore next time you shouldn't leave him so long.

Once he is happy for 10 minutes, you can call him over and give him a command to go in his crate, such as 'kennel', 'crate,' or 'den.' When he goes in the crate, give him praise and a treat, and close the door. Sit quietly nearby for a few minutes, then go to another room for a few minutes, then come back and sit next to the crate again for a few minutes before letting him out. Once you have increased the time to 30 minutes, you can start crating him when you leave the house. You should vary the point at which you leave every time, sometimes crating just before you leave, other times crating him five to 15 minutes prior. He is likely to be excited to see you when you come home, however don't reward him with acting excited yourself. Arrivals should be low-key, otherwise it reinforces his anxiety at you leaving.

You can also use the crate at night, starting from a puppy. Some owners prefer to place the crate near where they are sleeping at night initially. When he is sleeping soundly in the crate, it can then be moved to a location of your choice.

Housebreaking

"Consistency. Patience. Opportunity. Observation. These are critical for house training a puppy. You need to be prepared to be very observant and learn the cues your puppy gives when he has to go potty. Provide frequent potty break opportunities outside and use the same location every time. Be patient with the process. It takes time and can be one of the most frustrating details of raising a puppy."

Rochelle Woods
Spring Creek Labradoodles

Labradoodles are quick learners, so housebreaking your puppy should not be a problem. If you have an older dog that soils the house, or your dog reverts to soiling indoors after having been housebroken, it is worth consulting your vet as there may be an underlying physical problem. Otherwise it may be a psychological reaction to a stress factor in your dog's life, and you will need to find out the cause.

Dogs are born with a primal instinct to keep the area they sleep in clean. This makes crate training your new puppy an excellent idea to help with housebreaking, as you will be working with his natural instincts to have some control over his bladder and bowels, which are physically weak as a puppy.

Because your Labradoodle puppy does not yet have full control of his bodily functions, you need to recognize that keeping him confined to his crate for more than a couple hours during the day may cause him a lot of stress, because he will want to void but will be instinctively reluctant to soil his bed. Whenever you let your puppy out of his crate, he will be ready to urinate. You can capitalize on this by taking him straight out to the yard. Then use the command word, "Busy," "Peepees," or whatever you choose. Then, when he goes, praise and treat him for being so clever!

You should not use the command until your dog is just about to do the action you require. This way he learns to associate the word with the action alone, and not with sniffing or running around the yard.

Other times you can anticipate your dog's urge to void, whether or not you are crate training, is first thing in the morning and after eating. These are opportunities to teach him the command word in association with the action. Also, especially with male dogs, if you notice him sniffing where another animal has been, he may be just about to cover it with his own urine, so you can anticipate this and use the command word just as he cocks his leg.

This scent marking can also be useful at bedtime, as your dog may be reluctant to comply with voiding his bladder to your timetable, but a walk around the block will give him many opportunities!

Once your dog has learned your command word, you can take him out to the yard at regular intervals, and before you have to go out or put him in his crate. Then you will know that he is comfortable.

You should never scold your dog for accidents in the house. Usually, you are at fault for not having taken your puppy outside often enough. If you actually catch him in the act, a firm "No" will suffice, followed by whisking him outdoors whether or not he has finished the job. Otherwise, if you just discover a puddle on the floor, he will not know why he is being scolded, and you may make him stress incontinent.

You should clean any accidents thoroughly with an enzymatic pet cleaner to neutralize ammonia. This will avoid repeat soiling where a dog is drawn

Photo Courtesy of
Bobbie Couch

to cover the smell of ammonia. Beware of general household cleaners that contain this ingredient. A carpet shampooer may be your best friend if you do not have hard floors, and see you through the stressful weeks when your dog is not completely potty trained. This should not be long with a smart Labradoodle!

"Potty training is different for every pup. Just because your pups litter mate learned how to ring a bell to go outside in 2 days, don't stress if yours is still having a few accidents a few weeks in. Also change in diet, environment and schedule could cause stress that may manifest itself in extra whining and more accidents. This is normal. Prepare for this with extra patience and a good stain remover."

Jenny Williams
Happy Go Lucky Labradoodles

Recall

The best exercise your Labradoodle can have is an off-leash walk where he has plenty of space to run and lots of smells to discover. In order to enjoy this privilege, he needs good recall for his own safety.

It is best to teach your Labradoodle to come back on command without the constant focus of a ball or toy, since you won't always have one with you. That way he can use his brain to enjoy the stimuli around him, and exercise his body at a more healthy pace. If you are lucky enough to have access to a secure field, this is ideal for recall training. Otherwise you can begin in your backyard, or use a long training line in an open space.

When you begin recall training, you will need a good stock of treats which you can keep in a fanny-pack for convenience. You need to maintain your dog's attention amid all the competing distractions around him, so it is important to use lots of vocal encouragement, and a steady stream of treats to encourage your dog to stay with you.

Keep changing the direction you are traveling in, to encourage your dog's focus, calling him to you as you turn. And if he drifts away, call him back with his name and the command "Come." Shower him with praise for coming back.

If the worst happens, and your dog bolts away from you, it is tempting to run after him. This is a mistake, as your dog thinks it is a game of chase, and it gives him the upper hand. Instead you need to keep your nerve, which is why a secure field or park is advisable as you know your dog cannot actually escape. Stay where you are or even walk in the opposite direction. Eventually, your dog will notice and be unnerved at the space between you. At this point he will race back, which you have anticipated, calling "Come" to convey the message that returning is your idea, not his. In racing back, he is effectively obeying, and you can praise and treat him accordingly! Never chastise him for having run off, because at this point, he has returned, and he will think he is being told off for it!

Most Labradoodles will respond well to recall training as they are an intelligent breed that love their humans.

Bad Behavior

"A lot of Labradoodles unfortunately, are allowed to get away with certain behavior , which may seem small (or cute) at the time, but this eventually leads to more problematic issues. Counter surfing is one I hear a lot of. This one in part, I believe, is due to feeding them people food. They think it's their food up there and they just need to jump up on the counter to get it. They didn't know that juicy T Bone steak didn't have their name on it! First, no more people food, and a strip of duct tape, sticky side up, along the edge of the counter is sometime enough to discourage this bad habit, especially after getting it stuck on their paw a few times."

Jenny Williams
Happy Go Lucky Labradoodles

The best way to avoid undesirable behavior is early socialization and training. In most cases, the breeder will have already started the process before you bring your puppy home. But if you are adopting an adult dog with ingrained behaviors, you will have more of a challenge breaking bad habits. Nevertheless, there are strategies you can try at home before calling in a trainer.

Barking

"Some behaviors that are harder to deal with are play biting and ex-cessive barking. Not all puppies will display these traits, but if they do, the earlier you correct it the better. A time out in a kennel is an acceptable way to address barking for no reason, but it is likely there is a reason, and steps should be taken to rule out a real need or desire for attention. Biting should be replaced with chew toys as a first step."

Jeana Bigelow
Blue Ridge Labradoodles

Your Labradoodle may bark more than the average dog due to his Poo-dle genes. Barking is not a bad behavior in a dog, as it is a natural expres-sion of his own voice. It can even be a positive behavior, alerting the house-hold to the presence of an intruder, or alerting about drugs or biological evidence at a crime scene. However, for most owners, excessive barking can be very wearing, and can even lead to complaints from the neighbors. So, training your Labradoodle when to use his bark is important.

The key thing to bear in mind when training your dog not to bark inap-propriately is showing him the meaning of 'quiet.' Since the sound of your voice is effectively human barking to your dog, shouting at him to stop bark-ing when he is in full throttle will only encourage him more. Therefore, a calm approach to bark training is required. Many dog trainers believe in the value of clicker training for all taught commands, but it is especially useful for barking. This is because of the acute focus it sends to your dog's brain, with a clear signal that he has done the right thing, and can expect a re-ward. When your dog is actively barking at the postman or the neighbor's cat, don't raise your voice or even react, but wait for a meaningful break in his barking, then click and treat. This way you are rewarding the positive behavior. Don't expect instant results, but keep up this routine at every op-portunity until your Labradoodle realizes the behavior you want is 'Quiet.'

Other trainers adopt the approach that in order for your dog to un-derstand the difference between barking and quiet, you need to teach him to bark on command. So if he has not been commanded to bark, he is re-quired to stay quiet. This is the "Speak" command, which should be given when your dog purposefully barks once, while making eye contact with you, and rewarded with the clicker and a treat. You can then teach "Quiet" by clicking and treating when he is not using his voice, until he knows the dif-ference. Teaching "Speak" is a slightly riskier method of training out inappropriate barking, as your dog may bark for a treat if your training has been anything less than one hundred percent effective.

Some owners may, in desperation, resort to extreme devices such as anti-bark collars which release a citronella spray or mild electric shock when a dog barks. This method is not recommended as it creates a nervous and confused dog. Indeed, these devices are now illegal in some countries. Other similar methods that may seem less cruel, such as carrying a water spray or an aerosol containing compressed air, are still incompatible with positive reward-based training, which is widely accepted as the most effective way of training your family dog and building a bond of trust.

*Photo Courtesy of
Amy Miller*

Aggression

Aggression is not a trait associated with the Labradoodle, so if your dog shows any signs of it, there will be a reason.

Sometimes a Labradoodle puppy is not simply a happy mix of Labrador Retriever and Poodle, but he has the genetics of another breed or breeds in the mix. This is especially the case with many Australian Labradoodles. In these cases, the traits of the other breeds may randomly come through in the puppy, even several generations down the line. Labradoodles sometimes have Spaniel in the mix, and Spaniels can be prone to rage syndrome, so this may account for a Labradoodle that sometimes switches off and snaps.

Other times, a Labradoodle may be the product of casual breeding, where the parents have not been carefully selected for their impeccable temperaments. If you are buying a puppy and have done your homework, hopefully you should have avoided this pitfall. But if you have adopted a dog from a shelter, you may find he has genetic aggression issues that have led to his surrender. If you know the breeder, you should always inform them that their dog is aggressive, so that they can look at their breeding program and stop producing from lines where this tendency arises.

Sometimes a Labradoodle may be born with a perfect non-aggressive nature, but may sadly experience cruelty during his early life, creating a reactive dog who snaps out of fear. Dogs are incredibly forgiving, and Labradoodles are naturally drawn to humans, so a dog that has learned aggression may be turned around with sensitive, positive reinforcement training and a lot of love. This will take patience, time, and understanding, but will build a bond of trust as your dog learns to relax and enjoy life again.

Retraining a Labradoodle with aggression issues should never be attempted in a household with young children. This is especially for their own safety, but also because one-to-one attention works best in building trust. If your Labradoodle puppy shows aggression, other than having his normal tolerances pushed too far by a toddler, you should return him to the breeder. No rescue will rehome a dog prone to aggression where there are children in the household. If you do find yourself in this situation, the original rescue, or another one, should rehome the dog more appropriately.

Happily, in almost all cases, you will not experience aggression from your Labradoodle, as they are bred to be family dogs with an unswerving loyalty to their humans. If any of these behavior traits emerge in your dog, a dog trainer will be able to assess your pet and set you on the right path.

CHAPTER 9
Exercise and Work

"In a perfect scenario a Labradoodle needs about 60 minutes of exercise a day. This could be a walk or jog, playing fetch, walking on a treadmill, or playing in a backyard. The key to exercise is to stimulate their mind while working out their body. If you do the same walk and or always on a treadmill the dog will become bored and you won't receive the full benefit of the exercise. Make things interesting. Take different paths, explore new areas, be erratic on your directions so the dog always has to watch you and pay attention. In the end, the dog wants to explore...be adventurous with them!"

Robby Gilliam
Mountain View Labradoodles

Photo Courtesy of
Brenda Patterson

Photo Courtesy of
Zoe Wilson

Exercise Needs

"Some Labradoodles will require more exercise than others. In general, plan on at least two good walks a day with your dog, and a hearty play session or two. For those who have more energy to burn off, provide toys and bones that require them to think or to work at getting a little treat out of them."

Rochelle Woods
Spring Creek Labradoodles

You may have brought a Labradoodle into your life in anticipation of long country walks, and your dog will love you for it – but not until he is fully grown!

In fact, the best insurance for a healthy adult dog is moderate and gentle exercise during the puppy stage when his bones, tendons, ligaments, and joints are still soft and developing. But whatever his life stage, two walks a day are ideal.

So how much exercise should you give your Labradoodle puppy? As a general rule, five minutes for each month of his age, twice a day. So your two-month-old new arrival only needs a 10-minute walk twice a day, but as he does not yet have full immunity, his exercise needs can be satisfied in the yard. At three months he will enjoy two short 15-minute walks, and at six months he can have two half-hour walks. By one year of age, when your Labradoodle is an adult dog, two one-hour walks will keep him physically fit as well as exercising his active brain.

Agility and Flyball

HELPFUL TIP
Service Dog SOS

If you are approached by an unattended service dog, the dog is requesting that you follow them because their owner may be in distress. Service dogs are trained to get help if their owner is having a medical emergency. The dog may not bark or whine, but will likely nudge your leg to get your attention.

Labradoodles love to use their mind, tackle challenges, and try new things, so they are ideally suited to agility and flyball.

Although competing in Kennel Club licensed agility shows requires a dog to be registered, Labradoodles are still accepted on the Activity Register in the UK, and AKC Canine Partners in the US.

The Kennel Club website is useful for finding an agility or flyball class in your area. The local Labradoodle breed club or your veterinarian should also be able to help. Or you may know other dogs who compete in these activities, and who can recommend their club.

Your dog will not be able to compete in agility or flyball until he is 18 months old, but classes will accept dogs once they are fully grown at 12 months. Initially, the jumps and obstacles your dog will be trained to navigate will be low-impact, to protect his joints. As he progresses, he will be officially measured for competition and placed in size-appropriate classes. Agility is great fitness training for both you and your dog, and forges a strong partnership.

If you have any personal mobility issues, flyball may be better suited to you, as the dog is sent down the racing lane on his own as part of a relay team. At the end, the dog triggers a pedal, releasing a tennis ball, which he catches and returns to base! Your clever Labradoodle should soon pick this up and will have great fun.

Whatever direction your training takes you, communicating effectively with your dog sets him up for a lifetime of fun opportunities, as well as ensuring his safety. It is the best investment you can make in giving your Labradoodle his best life and building the bond between you.

Photo Courtesy of
Carrie Tropea

Assistance Dogs

Photo Courtesy of Kelly Lindloff

In the early years of the breed, Labradoodles were mostly simple hybrid crosses. However, the subsequent development of multigenerational Labradoodles has produced a breed that is more reliably hypoallergenic, making it well suited to assistance and therapy roles in households with allergies and asthma. The Labradoodle's non-shedding coat and low odor is a bonus. Multigenerational Labradoodles are also regarded as less boisterous than straight Labrador Poodle hybrids, which is an advantage in service dogs.

Labradoodles are now a popular choice as hearing dogs for the deaf, alerting their owners to important sounds such as the doorbell, the telephone, or the smoke alarm. They also fulfill an important role in giving their deaf owners a sense of confidence and companionship.

Guide dogs and hearing dogs are usually bred and trained by professionals, and placed with their recipient once fully trained at around a year. But for some other therapy roles, the Labradoodle puppy may grow up in the family home. One example is as a companion for a child with autism. The warm and friendly nature of the Labradoodle has made the breed a popular emotional anchor for autistic children, and being around a puppy from an early age helps their bond to grow. However, many advise that it's best for a dog to be raised by a breeder or trainer for the first few months, at least until the puppy is housebroken and has some basic training in place. The puppy should be well socialized and exposed to a variety of sights, sounds, and experiences from an early age, to ensure that the dog is comfortable and relaxed in its role as a service dog.

Not all therapy dogs are bred for a specific role. In many cases, Labradoodle owners recognize qualities in their dog that they feel make them an excellent candidate to visit the elderly in nursing homes, children in special schools, or the chronically sick in hospices. Interacting with a friendly dog

Preparations for Travel

Most dogs adapt well to traveling if it's something they've been used to since puppyhood. However, if you have a dog that finds the experience stressful, or you don't often travel with your Labradoodle in a car, you may have to spend a little time getting him accustomed to it without actually going anywhere. To do this, just allow your dog to explore the car at his own pace. Leave some treats in the car for him to find, and encourage him in a calm and positive voice. You may need to repeat this regularly before your planned trip.

Whether you are just traveling a few miles for a country walk, or going on vacation, you should make sure your dog is carrying some form of identification in case he gets lost. A collar and identity tag are great, but a microchip is ideal, as this cannot become detached from your dog. Do make sure your contact information is up to date with the company that registers your dog's microchip though, especially your cell phone number. If you are going on vacation, some owners like to attach a temporary tag to their dog's collar with their vacation address, as this can sometimes speed up the dog being reunited.

HELPFUL TIP
BringFido

When traveling with your loyal hound, you'll want to make sure that your accommodations will also be accommodating for your pet. While a typical travel agent may not be able to guarantee that your vacation is pet-friendly, there is now a service offering online support for planning your next dog-friendly trip. BringFido was founded by Melissa Halliburton, who was frustrated by the lack of pet policy information on hotel websites. BringFido offers travel support to locations around the world, and from campsites to hotels. For more information about this service, visit www.bringfido.com or call 877-411-FIDO.

If you are traveling a long distance or going to be away for a while, you may need to take your dog to your veterinarian for a health check before he travels. This gives you an opportunity to ask about region-specific illnesses which might not be prevalent in your area. For example, warmer climates often have more ticks, and wetter climates might have more lungworm. It's also worth researching the veterinary practices in the area you will be visiting, as you never know when you may need to get to a vet in an emergency. Program the phone numbers of some local vets into your cell phone, in case you can't get an internet signal when you need it. Also ensure that you have your regular vet's number programmed into your phone, as the emergency vet may need your dog's medical history.

Traveling in a Car

"Labradoodles are extremely social and want to be with their family. They love to be on the go with you and doing whatever you are doing. They make excellent traveling companions as long as you train them to travel well in a car and to be calm on a leash."

Rochelle Woods
Spring Creek Labradoodles

In many countries, such as the UK, it's illegal to travel with your dog in the car if he's unrestrained or uncontained. In any case, it's common sense that you need to ensure your dog can't jump around in a moving car, or be thrown out of the car if an accident occurs. It may also invalidate your vehicle and/or pet insurance to travel with a dog loose in the car. So, to travel with your Labradoodle safely, you need to make a choice between a crate, a dog guard, or a travel harness.

Photo Courtesy of
Blair Brainard

If your Labradoodle is crate-trained, this is an advantage, as he already sees a crate as a safe space in which he can settle down and relax. This means he will be less prone to stress and travel sickness. It also means you will know he is safely contained, and that he is not making a mess of your car.

You can use your dog's regular crate for travel by transferring it to the car, but most owners who travel with their Labradoodles regularly find it more convenient to have a separate crate for the car. Depending on your make of vehicle, you may find that a crate with a slanting front fits better in the hatch than a square crate. Or you may even have a crate custom-fitted to your car. You can put a bed, blankets, or towels in the crate for your dog's comfort.

If you don't want to use a crate, you can opt to fit a dog guard between your back seats and the hatch of the car. Many dog guards are adjustable to fit most vehicles, or you can purchase one that has been made for your car. The advantage of a custom fit is that the dog will not have gaps to rest his chin while he drools down the back seats! A custom-fitted hatch liner is also a good idea if you want to keep your vehicle in good condition.

Another option for traveling with your Labradoodle in the car is a dog harness. These fit securely around the dog's chest, and attach to the seat belt. Even if your dog protests initially at the restraint, he will soon get used to the idea, and settle down on the back seat. However, you may want to cover your seat, especially if you're taking your Labradoodle for a muddy walk.

Travel sickness may not always result in vomiting, but if your dog drools excessively in the car or smacks his lips, this may be a sign that he is experiencing nausea. If your dog gets travel sick, always travel him on an empty stomach. Your vet can also prescribe travel sickness medication, which you will need to give half an hour before setting out.

Above all, think of your dog's comfort when you travel. This includes bedding, access to water, and regular opportunities to relieve himself. Many dogs can't cope with food on a journey, so this is not a priority. However, if your journey is a very long one, your dog will need time to eat and digest a small meal at least every 12 hours. Also be mindful of temperatures if your vehicle isn't air conditioned, ideally choosing the most comfortable time of day to travel, depending on your climate.

Finally, always remember, dogs can die very quickly if left in a hot car with the windows closed, as the temperature inside can rise much quicker than you think. If you need to leave the car, take your dog with you if at all possible, but if you have to leave your dog for a brief moment, be sure you're parked in the shade and there is adequate fresh airflow to where he is sitting.

Photo Courtesy of
Melissa Rodriguez

Traveling by Plane

It's never ideal to travel a dog by plane, but sometimes it has to be done, such as if you're moving house. Also, with a breed such as the Labradoodle, some breeders ship their puppies abroad to their new homes.

There's a lot to think about when traveling your dog by air.

In some cases, small dogs can travel in the cabin, as long as their crate fits under the seat. However, most adult Labradoodles are too large for this arrangement, so they will have to travel as cargo, the exception being service dogs, which can travel with their owners.

Whether he's traveling in the cabin or cargo, your dog will need a flight-approved crate, big enough for him to stand up and move around in. You should check the maximum dimensions with your airline. The crate should have a sign saying "Live Animal," and a label with your name, address, cell phone number, and contact information for your destination. A photo of your dog should also be attached to avoid any mix-ups, and your dog should also wear an identity tag bearing the same information. Don't lock the crate, as the airport staff may need to open it. It's usual for a dog to travel on an empty stomach, but you should attach a small bag of food to the crate in case of any long delays, so the airline staff can feed him if necessary.

Many owners feel a lot more confident using a specialist pet carrier service to make all the arrangements for the flight. Usually this will involve booking you and your dog onto the same flight. Usually the service also provides a crate. If you don't fly often with your dog, employing a professional service can save you money and give you peace of mind.

If you're making your own arrangements, you should first research your flight thoroughly, avoiding plane transfers and busy holiday periods if possible. In warm climates, you should aim to fly during the cooler part of the day, and in cold climates, aim for the middle of the day. You will probably need to make your booking with the airline by phone rather than online, to ensure that your dog can travel on the flight you have in mind, and that there is space for both of you on the same flight.

If you're traveling internationally and are going to need a pet passport, think ahead, as some vaccinations such as rabies require time to take effect and be validated by a blood test.

With your booking made, you should make an appointment with your vet for a health check at least 30 days prior to your flight. Your vet will issue

Photo Courtesy of Courtney Nadeau

a certificate stating that your dog is fit to fly and up-to-date with his vaccinations. If you're making a return journey, and this falls beyond the 30-day validity period of your health certificate, you will need to make another appointment to get a new certificate while you're away.

Sedatives are not usually recommended for dogs traveling by plane, as they can increase the risk of heart or respiratory issues caused by atmospheric pressure. They can also cause a loss of balance, making your dog feel unwell.

Before you travel, it's important to research the forecasted temperatures at that time of year. If it's below 45 degrees Fahrenheit or above 85 degrees Fahrenheit during departure, arrival, and connections, for his own safety your dog may not be allowed to travel. This is unless you can provide a letter from your veterinarian confirming your dog is frequently subjected to these temperatures, and therefore is used to them.

Vacation Lodging

Most Labradoodles will love to join you on your vacation, simply because they want to be with you at all times, but especially if your destination involves exploring the countryside or swimming in the sea. And for many families, a vacation just isn't the same without their dog's exuberant participation!

So, the first thing many owners do when booking their vacation is to look for accommodations that will accept dogs. It's important to check whether a dog the size of a Labradoodle is welcome at your intended hotel or self-catering lodge, as some holiday accommodations will only allow small dogs.

When you arrive at your destination, check the visitor information pack for the house rules. It's likely that your dog will not be allowed on the furniture or the bed. He may also not be allowed upstairs if the accommodations are on more than one floor. It's important to respect the rules, as your dog is a guest in someone else's property that will also be used by many other people. You should not leave your dog home alone in a vacation property, as he may be more unsettled in an unfamiliar place, and bark or be destructive. If you're really organized, you can look up local dog sitters for your vacation area, in case you want to go out for a family meal or excursion where dogs are not allowed.

Always make sure you leave the property in the same state as you found it. The Labradoodle's low-shedding coat is in your favor, since you should be able to leave a hotel or rental without any trace of your dog ever having been there!

Photo Courtesy of
Allison Moore

Leaving Your Dog at Home

If you're traveling abroad for your vacation, you will probably choose to leave your Labradoodle at home, in which case there are several options open to you.

Many owners are lucky enough to have a trusted friend or family member who is willing to look after their dog, either at their place or yours. If your dog will be boarding at your friend's home, ensure that their yard is fully secure, and leave your friend with your dog's bed or crate, his leash, toys, and bowls, and enough of his regular food for the time you're away. You may wish to portion the food out in bags to make life easier. Written instructions will also be helpful, especially if your dog is on any medication, and you should include contact information for where you're staying, as well as details of your local vet.

If your friend has a dog of their own, make sure the dogs know each other before yours comes to visit. Take them for walks on neutral territory, so that the resident dog does not feel defensive toward your dog when he's obliged to share his home and his humans. This arrangement often works well for dog owners, as the favor can be reciprocated.

If you don't have a friend or family member who can look after your dog, you may decide to use the services of a professional. Again, this may be at their place or yours. If your dog is to board in the pet sitter's home, it's likely to be well set up for dogs. However, there may be other dogs there at the same time, so your dog should be sociable (not usually a problem for Labradoodles), and up-to-date with his vaccinations. If the pet sitter stays in your home, this may be more costly, but your dog will be settled in his familiar place, and your home will also be looked after while you are away.

Finally, you may choose to book your Labradoodle into boarding kennels. If you haven't used kennels before, it's worth asking dog-owning friends for recommendations. You will enjoy your vacation more if you know that other friends' dogs have had a good experience in the kennels of your choosing.

The staff at boarding kennels are professionals with a lot of experience in dog care and managing ailments. Your dog will probably stay in a kennel divided into two sections, a sheltered sleeping area, and an outdoor run. He will be taken out for a walk once or twice a day, and probably allowed to play in a communal area. If you choose a kennel for your dog, he will need to have an up-to-date vaccination record, including kennel cough.

Labradoodles are generally easygoing dogs that will adapt well to whatever arrangement you make for them. However, they are very much individuals, so only you will know what is best for your dog. Whether you're traveling a few short miles to the vet or the park, taking your dog on a long journey by car or plane, going on vacation with him, or making arrangements for him to stay behind, a bit of forward planning can make this part of dog ownership easier for you both!

CHAPTER 11
Nutrition

Importance of Nutrition

Nutrition is vitally important to keep your Labradoodle in top condition. While your Labradoodle probably will eat anything, you are responsible for ensuring he only has access to good nutrition. Nutrition is closely related to the health of the skin, coat, eyes, brain, nerves, immune system, gut, kidneys, and heart, so it's worth paying attention to! In this chapter, we will look at what sort of food is available on the market, and what is best for your Labradoodle.

Photo Courtesy of
Chrystal Sanchez

Types of Food

You'll probably find the supermarket or pet store shelves rather over-whelming at first. There are many different types of food, from wet to dry, different flavors, different manufacturers, and a variety of prices. So how do you know which one to choose?

As a good starting point, if you have a puppy, it is best to continue him on the food the breeder has placed him on for the first few weeks. This is because a puppy's stomach can be prone to stress, and so to make the transition into a new house as smooth as possible, continuing the diet he is used to is best. After a few weeks of the old food, you can transition him onto the food of your choice.

So, when you go to the pet store, the first choice to make is wheth-er you wish to start your puppy on a wet or a dry food. Both have their advantages and disadvantages, and many owners will choose to feed a mixture of both. Wet food is much more palatable than dry food, and dogs with a fussy appetite may prefer it. This is unlikely to be a prob-lem though, if your Labradoodle has inherited a Labrador's appetite! Wet food also usually has a higher protein content than dry food, which is more natural for a dog. Dry food, on the other hand, usually has a higher carbohydrate content, which is not as close to the diet of your dog's an-cestors, though many dogs still do very well on it. The positive side about dry food is that kibble helps to clean a dog's teeth and may prevent den-tal disease later in life.

Other types of food to look out for are life-stage and breed-size-specif-ic. All growing puppies should be given a puppy food. This is much higher in protein, calcium, and phosphorus for those growing muscles and bones. Old dogs should be given a senior food. Senior recipes have fewer calories, for a more sedentary lifestyle, as well as more omega oils to help with joint and heart health. There are also types of food for different sizes of dogs. If you have bought a miniature Labradoodle, then he may benefit from a small-breed dog food. Likewise, if your Labradoodle grows to over 60lbs, he will be best on a large-breed dog food. As well as kibble size, these different types of food related to breed size, will have slightly different formulations of minerals, vitamins, proteins, and carbohydrates, to address the growth and metabolism differences between the sizes.

Photo Courtesy of
Delaney Price

How to Choose a Good Food

Now that we have addressed the different types of diets, and you've narrowed down what sort of food you want, you'll probably still be presented with several brands which all meet your criteria. There are several ways to assess the quality of the dog food by simply looking at the label, including looking at information about the ingredients and guaranteed analysis.

Ingredients

All dog foods must have a comprehensive ingredients list on the packaging. The ingredients are listed in order of weight, which means the first ingredient on the list makes up the largest proportion in the recipe. This can sometimes be a little confusing, as lamb, for example, contains a lot of water, so even though it may be the heaviest ingredient, it may not be the main contributor to protein in the diet. Likewise, dehydrated meat, known as 'meal,' such as chicken meal, contains 300 percent more protein than the same weight of its hydrated form.

When looking at the ingredients list, you want to find a food which has a meat protein source as the main ingredient. This is the most natural food for a dog. Other ingredients in the recipe should be carbohydrates and vegetables, with minimal chemical additives. Vegetables in particular are excellent sources of vitamins A, B, and C, as well as magnesium, potassium, and iron. In combination, this will help keep the eyes and brain healthy, keep the heart beating in a regular rhythm, boost the immune system, improve the production of red blood cells, and aid in nerve conduction.

Some people choose not to feed their dogs diets containing grain. There is some early evidence that grains may contribute to skin allergies and heart conditions, however the scientific evidence at this stage is currently lacking, and the reality is most dogs tolerate grains very well. If your dog does tolerate grains, they can be an excellent source of dietary fiber which will keep your dog's bowel movements regular.

Lastly, one ingredient in particular which you will want to ensure your Labradoodle is getting is an ingredient high in omega oils. Omega oils may not be directly listed on the ingredients list, but they can be found in oily ingredients such as fish and seeds. Omega oils are particularly important for Labradoodles for two reasons; firstly, they help keep their coats looking healthy and shiny, and secondly, they help to improve the health of the joints, which can be a breed issue in Labradoodles.

HELPFUL TIP
Puppy Food

The dog food aisle at your local pet store can be confusing. You may wonder when it's appropriate to feed your dog puppy food and when you'll want to switch to adult food. The general rule of thumb is to feed your dog puppy food until he or she is 12 months old before making the switch to adult dog food. Talk to your veterinarian about the correct serving sizes and frequency for your particular dog as nutritional needs will change during your dog's first year of life.

Guaranteed Analysis

As per the AAFCO (American Association of Feed Control Officials) guidelines, all pet food labels must contain a guaranteed analysis. This is a breakdown of the constituents of the food; carbohydrates, proteins, fiber, ash, moisture, and fats. This is only useful in combination with looking at the ingredients; however, it can give a valuable insight into how nutritious the food is. These details are per gram of ready-to-eat food, and therefore two diets cannot be directly compared without first doing some calculations.

For example, if a wet food is 75 percent wet, then it means the dry content is 25 percent. If the protein level is then five percent, this can be converted by dividing by the dry matter percentage: 5/0.25 = 20 percent protein on a dry matter basis. Then if a similar dry food, which you wanted to compare, had a moisture content of 10 percent and a dry content of 90 percent, with a protein level of 20 percent, the calculation would be as follows: 20/0.9 = 22.2 percent protein on a dry matter basis.

BARF And Homemade Diets

Raw food, and less commonly, cooked homemade diets, are becoming increasingly popular, despite being controversial. Many people who feed their dogs raw food are firm believers in the benefits, and will strongly defend their choice. They claim their dogs' health has improved as well as its coat, skin, teeth, and general energy and demeanor, and firsthand experiences and pre- and post-diet change photos can certainly be persuasive. Nevertheless, the benefits of the diet are still very much in the anecdotal stages, so if you are considering it for your Labradoodle, make sure you thoroughly do your research beforehand and consult a veterinary nutritionist first.

Raw food diets first came onto the scene in 1993, when a veterinarian named Ian Billinghurst, from Australia, suggested that it would be best to feed a diet closer to the natural food a dog would eat in the wild. The type of diet was called 'BARF,' which stood for 'Bones and Raw Food' or 'Biologically Appropriate Raw Food.' BARF diets tend to be made up of uncooked meat, whole or crushed uncooked bones, raw eggs, vegetables, and fruit. Billinghurst was adamant that this type of diet would be more beneficial for the health of domesticated dogs, and he was vocal about his views against commercial dog food. However, this is a view that most vets now do not support.

There have now been numerous studies on raw food demonstrating the high numbers of dangerous pathogens which can be transmitted to dogs, and their owners, from these diets. These pathogens include bacteria such as salmonella, E.coli, and campylobacter. Not only do they stay in the saliva of your dog, but they are also still present in the feces and coat when your dog grooms himself. This means the bacteria can be readily transmitted to people. At particular risk are those people who are more vulnerable,

such as children and the elderly. In these age groups, infections with these pathogens can be life-threatening. Dogs also can develop illness from infections which derive from these pathogens, although generally the gastrointestinal system of a dog is significantly more robust than that of a human and therefore, many dogs can withstand some level of contact without developing a disease. Meticulous hygiene during preparation can mitigate some of the risk. Disinfecting the area where the food was prepared, your hands, and your dog's bowl after every use will decrease these harmful pathogens in the environment considerably.

There are other risks which come with BARF diets which contain whole bones. Bones can present risks of choking, damage to teeth, internal punctures, and internal obstructions. Most raw food advocates will argue that raw bones are more flexible and digest better than cooked bones, but regardless, there is still some element of risk.

Finally, the main concern by veterinarians is the difficulty of balancing BARF and homemade diets appropriately. In a study of 95 homemade dogfood diets, 60 percent were found to have a major nutritional deficiency. The majority of homemade food feeders haven't consulted an expert veterinary nutritionist, but rather have developed their dog's diet through personal research or advice from breeders or friends who also feed their dogs raw or homemade diets. As a result, the diet is not balanced properly, and there are excessive levels of calcium and phosphorus or incorrect levels of other nutrients. This can lead to serious consequences in a dog such as rickets, bladder stones, and stunted growth, particularly if the animal is not yet fully grown.

Nevertheless, there are some suppliers of raw food in the commercial market, which have started to produce products which can mitigate many of these potential pitfalls. Though vets tend to universally agree that homemade raw food has the potential to be exceptionally dangerous, many will now accept commercially produced products. This is because these products are tested to ensure that the nutrients are correctly balanced. Many manufacturers also test their meat for pathogens, and therefore can certify that they are pathogen-free and safe for consumption.

Despite the obvious risks, many people are still driven toward homemade raw diets through anecdotal evidence, hype, and very persuasive pre- and post-diet change photographs. Unfortunately, a great number of these influencers are pedigree or designer dog breeders, passing on their passion to unknowledgeable first-time puppy owners who are not aware of the risks, so you should always do your own research.

Treats

Every owner loves to feed their dog. It's an easy way to their heart, especially the heart of a Labradoodle! However, giving your dog treats all the time is the same as giving your child sweets all the time; they are not as nutritious as regular food, and your dog doesn't need the extra calories. Occasional treats are fine, especially when training your Labradoodle, but try not to let it become excessive.

There are many different types of treats on the market, from small bite-sized training treats, to bones and antlers. It is best to stay away from treats which can cause blockages or splinter, such as cooked bones or rawhide chews, but antlers are great for your dog to gnaw on if you are looking for a delicious, long-lasting treat, and liver snaps are perfectly sized, natural, and nutritious rewards to use when training.

Always remember that treats contain calories, and therefore you should alter your dog's normal food calorie content for the day to reflect how many treats you have doled out.

Weight Monitoring

Monitoring your dog's weight is as important as monitoring your own. There is so much variation in the Labradoodle breed, though, that it is impossible to say that a Labradoodle should weigh a specific amount.

Therefore, the best way to monitor weight is not through figures, but instead, body condition scores. An ideal body condition score is 4 to 5, and the range goes from 1 (emaciated) to 9 (obese). The scores are standardized for anybody to use, and are easy and repeatable from dog to dog. Labradoodles will require hands-on assessing, as their luscious long fur may obscure the outline of the ribs, waist and abdominal tuck. These are the descriptions of the following scores:

BCS 1 =   Emaciated. Ribs, lumbar vertebral projections, and bony prominences around the pelvis are clearly visible. There is severe loss of muscle and no body fat.

BCS 3 =   Underweight. The ribs can be felt easily and might be visible. There's not much fat present. The abdomen tucks up at the flank and the waist can be seen from the top. Some bony projections can be seen. It's easy to see the top of the lumbar vertebrae.

BCS 5 =   Ideal. There's minimal fat over the ribs and they can easily be felt. The waist and ribs are visible when standing above the dog. The abdomen is tucked when viewed from the side.

BCS 7 =   Overweight. Fat is present over ribs and some pressure is required to feel them. There are fat deposits over the rump and around the tail base. The waist is not easily visible. The abdominal tuck present but slight.

BCS 9 =   Obese. There's lots of fat around the base of the tail, spine, and chest. The abdomen may bulge behind the ribs. No waist or abdominal tuck is visible. There are fat deposits on the neck and limbs.

If your Labradoodle is struggling with his weight despite regular appropriate exercise, it is best to try one of two approaches. First, you can alter their food intake by 10 percent. This is done by weighing out or measuring how much food you usually give, and then calculating the change. The other option is to feed the amount of food required, according to the packaging, based on a target weight. If you need some support, many vet practices will hold weigh-ins with their veterinary nurses, who can be an excellent source for encouragement and tips.

In the end, each Labradoodle is an individual, and therefore, there is not one perfect diet that will suit all Labradoodles. It is best to seek the help of professionals, such as canine or veterinary nutritionists, veterinary nurses or veterinarians, if you are not sure how to choose a diet for your dog to ensure that he is as healthy as can be.

CHAPTER 12
Grooming

"Grooming your Labradoodle can be a great bonding activity in addition to providing necessary coat maintenance. Keep the ear hair no longer than 1/2" longer than the ear leather, and the hair under the ear flap clipped short to allow good air flow. Keep chin hair trimmed neatly so they do not drip excessive water after drinking. Keep the hair around the front of the paws and in between the pads trimmed short to prevent dragging in a lot of dirt and debris. Do a "sanitary" clip to keep hair clean and free of urine or feces build up issues. Always keep the hair trimmed between the eyes, so vision is not obstructed."

Rochelle Woods
Spring Creek Labradoodles

Photo Courtesy of
Patricia Adams

Photo Courtesy of
Jan Armstrong

One of the main reasons you might be attracted to owning a Labradoodle is its beautiful coat and cute, cuddly appearance. Some Labradoodles have the advantage of being low-shedding, which means that they will not lose their coat. As a result, keeping the coat well-groomed is vital. As discussed earlier, Labradoodles come in a variety of coat types, and it's often only once they're a little older that you will truly know which one your Labradoodle will have. Whichever he ends up with, it will require some maintenance. As well as the coat, the ears, teeth, nails, and anal glands must all be maintained, to ensure that they do not impact on the overall health of your dog. This chapter will provide an overview of how to ensure your Labradoodle is well cared for from a grooming perspective.

Coat Types

"F1's are typically the 'Wash and Wear' least grooming needed. F2's, Multi Gens, and F1B's typically need daily brushing and routine groom- ing. Good rule of thumb: If it's already matted, it's too late. Better to shave and start over. Most doodle owners have a shorter 'Summer Cut' and by winter, it has grown back. Research your groomer and make sure they are familiar with the breed and cuts. Don't 'Poodle' your 'Doodle'."

Jenny Williams
Happy Go Lucky Labradoodles

The Labradoodle has three coat types; hair, fleece, or wool. These are large- ly influenced by the genetics of the parents. However, it's not impossible for ancestral genes to suddenly pop up and produce a puppy with an unexpect- ed coat type. F1 and early generation puppies are more likely to be variable in the litter. However, by purchasing a multigenerational Labradoodle, you can be more confident in what you're buying.

Hair Coat

The hair coat is similar to a Labrador's, although a little longer. It's often seen in the F1, F1b, and F2b generations. It can carry an odor and will shed to some degree.

Fleece Coat

The fleece coat is a soft-textured coat. It can either be a straight wave or a spiral curl. This is the coat that most Labradoodle breeders aim for, and is the one that most clients prefer because it's easier to manage than the oth- er types of coat, and is most likely to be hypoallergenic.

Wool Coat

The wool coat is very similar to a Poodle's coat. It's thick and dense and requires frequent grooming.

Brushing

"Many people believe that a Labradoodle will have an easy coat to care for, but the opposite is true. It requires a great deal of upkeep to keep it free of mats. Brushing several times a week is usually necessary, and it is important to check problem areas frequently for mats: behind the ears, under the tail, under the legs where they attach to the body, and under the collar."

Rochelle Woods
Spring Creek Labradoodles

Photo Courtesy of
Melissa Rodriguez

Regularly grooming your Labradoodle's coat is something that you should make time for. Most Labradoodles' coats are moderate or high maintenance, and therefore, even though a professional groomer can bathe, brush, and clip your Labradoodle once every four to six weeks, the coat will still require some home care.

Labradoodles' coats can become matted if they're not regularly brushed, and if you've purchased a Labradoodle which sheds his coat, brushing regularly will at least catch the loose hair and spare your carpet to some degree!

It's a good idea to establish a brushing routine early on, as then your Labradoodle will tolerate it better. You should check through your dog's coat two to three times every week, and brush any areas which have become knotted with a slicker brush. The most important areas to concentrate on are the armpits, behind the ears, chest, and neck. You should part the coat to the skin, and brush from the base of the coat. This will ensure you don't miss any matting close to the skin.

Bathing

FUN FACT
Guinness World Record

On September 4, 2014, an Australian Labradoodle named Ranmaru set the world record for longest eyelash on a dog. Ranmaru's right eyelash was measured in Chuo, Japan, and came in at 17 centimeters or 6.69 inches.

Bathing your dog is something you should do to keep his coat clean, especially if he has an affinity for dirty water like his Labrador ancestors. However, bathing too frequently can also be detrimental to his skin and coat, stripping them of their natural oils.

If you find your dog gets dirty after every walk, it's safe to rinse him off with warm water. This will not be detrimental to the coat. But now and then, you may find you need something a little more for cleanliness' sake and to remove any odor, especially if you have a hair-coated Labradoodle. In this case, a dog shampoo is appropriate, but ensure that you purchase a good quality dog shampoo that is kind to the skin. These often contain tea tree or oatmeal, and have minimal chemicals.

A shampoo bath should not be done more than once a month, and if you send your Labradoodle to the groomer's frequently, they will bathe your dog for you before they clip him.

Ear Cleaning

Ear cleaning is vital to ensure that your Labradoodle doesn't develop ear infections. In Chapter 14, we will look at how Labradoodles are prone to these. Cleaning the ears with a neutral ear cleaner a couple of times a month will help to remove all the wax and dirt which may accumulate. You can also use the ear cleaner after your Labradoodle has swum in dirty water, as this is also a place where he can easily pick up bacteria.

Cleaning the ears is a simple procedure, although one that can be messy. First, place the nozzle of the cleaner in the ear canal, and give a squirt of the product. Next, remove the bottle, and quickly place the flap of the ear over the exit of the ear canal to stop any cleaner from coming out. You can then gently massage the ear to ensure the cleaner makes its way down to the end of the ear canal. After ten seconds of massaging, you can let go of the ear and stand back. Your Labradoodle is bound to shake his head to rid the fluid from his ear, and with it will come any debris or wax which has accumulated in the canal. You can then wipe this away with some cotton wool.

Dental Care

Dental health is very closely related to general health, and therefore keeping your dog's teeth in good condition is vital. Dental care is something that many owners unknowingly neglect, and as a result, many older dogs have developed so much tartar build-up by their senior years that their mouths are uncomfortable and smelly. It's a myth that if your dog is eating well, his mouth is comfortable, and eating easily is not a reliable indicator of dental health.

Tartar, also known as plaque, is a mixture of leftover food material and bacteria which can accumulate on the teeth. When tartar collects close to the gums, it causes gingivitis which results in sore, bleeding gums. This can lead to the weakening of the periodontal ligaments, which hold teeth in the socket, and as a result, teeth may become wobbly and fall out.

Prevention is much better than cure, and there is a lot that can be done to prevent tartar build-up. Firstly, as previously discussed in Chapter 11, the type of food you feed your dog will influence how much gets stuck in between his teeth. Dry food provides some abrasion against the tooth, and in fact, cleans the tooth to some degree, whereas wet food is more likely to get stuck and cause tartar build-up. You can also feed your dog dental treats

Photo Courtesy of
Betsy Glennon

in moderation, which work based on the same principle; the abrasion helps to remove tartar. However, you should stay clear of treats like bones, which can splinter and cause obstructions. Deer antlers are an excellent alternative for gnawing on.

The main way you should keep your dog's mouth clean is by using dental products, such as dog toothpaste. Human toothpaste should never be used, as it can contain ingredients that are toxic to your Labradoodle. Dog toothpaste usually has a meaty flavor, which your dog will love, and it contains enzymes that help to dissolve tartar. Daily cleaning is vital, and you should introduce this to your dog at the age of a puppy, as otherwise, he may find it to be stressful. There is also dog mouthwash which you can use. You simply add it to your dog's water every day. It's important that human mouthwash is never used, as, like human toothpaste, it can be toxic and lead to liver damage. The water with added mouthwash should be completely replaced with fresh water daily. This will ensure the enzymes in the mouthwash are working efficiently. As with the toothpaste, the enzymes help to dissolve the tartar from the teeth. Mouthwash is less effective than brushing, however, and if your Labradoodle already has considerable tartar build-up, it will probably only prevent it from worsening, rather than treat the problem.

If you have an older dog, or if you've rescued a Labradoodle who has gone a large part of his life without dental care, you may find that the tartar build-up is now too much to manage with home care. In this case, your dog can have a dental procedure done at your local vet practice. It will require a short anesthetic, so your dog will need to be there in the morning. When your dog is asleep, the vet will scale and polish all his teeth, and then check them all for any pockets within the socket. This can be an indication that the periodontal ligament is deteriorating and that a tooth may need to be extracted. The wonderful things about dental procedures are that afterward, your dog's mouth will be comfortable, his breath fresh, and his teeth as pearly white as a puppy's.

Nail Trimming

Dogs have four nails on each paw, and on the front leg there is also a dewclaw on the inside. Some dogs may have dewclaws on the inside of their back legs too, but this is unusual. All these nails will need to be routinely clipped as they can tend to grow in a curved manner which then results in them damaging the underside of the paw, or being susceptible to being caught and causing toe sprains and dislocations.

Clipping nails can cause some dogs great anxiety, so teaching your dog to be still and not panic when young is a good idea. Start as a puppy by playing with your dog's paws and giving him plenty of praise when he doesn't fuss.

You can buy dog nail clippers from most pet stores, and these are far superior to using human nail clippers. Choose a size which is most appropriate for your size of Labradoodle.

The nail is made up of keratin, which does not contain nerves or blood vessels, so if you clip the nail correctly, it will not cause your dog any pain. However, running down the center of the nail is a fleshy section called the quick. If you accidentally cut the quick, it will bleed. This is not dangerous, merely uncomfortable for your dog. Simply apply firm pressure to it with a wad of cotton wool for five minutes to get it under control.

Knowing where the quick ends is usually a guessing game for dogs with black nails. However, if you're lucky to have a dog with clear nails, then it can easily be seen. For dogs with black nails, taking small bits off at a time, rather than one big cut is a better idea. You can also use a nail file to slowly grind down your dog's nails as these are less prone to damaging the quick, but this can take some time and requires some patience from your Labradoodle. You can purchase a battery-operated rotary nail-grinder to speed the process. If you're nervous about cutting your dog's nails, a groomer or a veterinary nurse will be more than happy to help you out.

Anal Glands

The anal glands are two sacs sitting just inside the anus. They have no functional purpose. Normally they have nothing in them because when a normal, firm stool passes them, they get squeezed, and if something has accumulated in them, it comes out. However, this can go wrong for two reasons. If they are anatomically in the wrong place, or if the stools which pass them are not firm, then fecal material begins to accumulate in them.

Photo Courtesy of Donna Hinde

When the anal glands get full, they become quite uncomfortable. Most dogs try to alleviate them by rubbing their behinds on the floor, known as scooting. Sometimes this provides enough pressure for them to express the material which has gotten stuck, but not always. If your dog gets very irritated by the discomfort, you may see him lick or bite at his anal area. Another indicator that your Labradoodle is suffering from full anal glands is an unmistakably fishy smell. This is pungent and you certainly won't miss it!

It's important to take your dog to the vet to have his anal glands expressed if he's suffering from these symptoms. Some groomers will also be able to empty them for you. However, it's better to go to the vet because if the glands have been impacted for a while, they may have become infected and need antibiotics. Leaving them full can be dangerous because if they become infected, they can form an abscess that can burst, which unsurprisingly is very painful.

If your Labradoodle has recurrent anal gland impactions or infections, this may sometimes be resolved with a diet change to create firmer stools. If this doesn't work, surgery is also an option to remove the glands, although this is not first-line treatment as the nerves which cause the anus to stay closed run very close to the anal glands, and if they are damaged during surgery, it can result in fecal incontinence.

It may seem that you have to consider a lot to keep your Labradoodle tidy, but once it becomes part of your routine, you will find it takes very little time at all and can be very satisfying. Grooming health can be closely related to general health, and so your Labradoodle will be grateful to you for keeping him in good condition.

CHAPTER 13
Preventative Health Care

Naturally, your top concern for your Labradoodle is likely to be his health. As you will learn in Chapter 14, the Labradoodle is prone to many inherited diseases, so it is worth being proactive when it comes to your dog's health. This chapter will discuss the routine preventative health measures which are recommended when owning a dog.

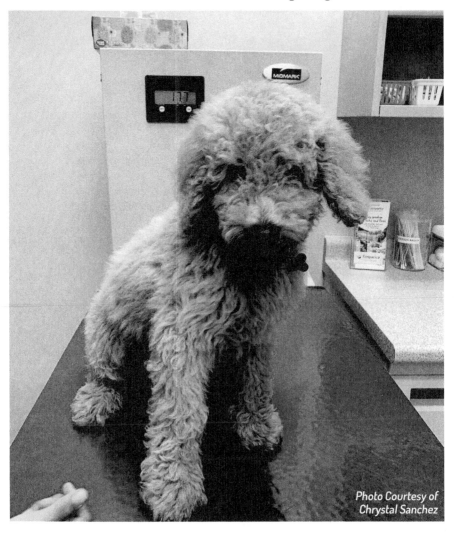

Photo Courtesy of Chrystal Sanchez

Choosing a Veterinarian

So, you've brought your new Labradoodle home. The next step is to also welcome a veterinarian into your family. A veterinarian should be chosen carefully, as many people keep the same veterinarian throughout their dog's life. This is beneficial, because the vet will then know your Labradoodle's medical history and personality, and you will learn to trust him with your dog. The last point is particularly important, as your Labradoodle is inevitably going to make their way into your heart as a child would. Therefore, you are sure to want someone who will take the utmost care of your Labradoodle.

There are many things to consider when choosing a veterinarian. Many people will choose the nearest veterinarian to them, to ensure that in the case of an emergency, they can get their pets to the vet swiftly. But there are also other factors to consider.

After Hours

Many veterinary practices are now outsourcing their after-hours emergency appointments to specialist emergency services; however, there are still some smaller independent practices who keep them in-house.

If a practice covers their after-hours emergency appointments, the advantage is that you will be seeing your normal veterinarian in a familiar setting, which may ease the tension of a highly stressful situation. In addition to this, your dog will have continuity of care throughout the day and night if he needs to be hospitalized.

On the other hand, if your vet practice outsources their after-hours emergency appointments to a specialist service, even though this will be unfamiliar to you, it will likely be provided by a veterinarian who is a specialist in emergency critical care.

Specialties

It is worth spending some time researching the qualifications of the staff, as you may find that some are qualified in specialist areas. This is advantageous to you as if your Labradoodle ever has any complicated issues, he may be able to be treated close to home at your local vet practice, rather than needing to be referred to a specialist center.

Photo Courtesy of Melissa Rodriguez

Extras

Many veterinary practices offer extra services which you may feel you don't need at this time, although you will be happy that they are there when you do need them. These include services such as puppy classes, weight management clinics, diabetic clinics, dental check-ups, and senior wellness checks.

Microchipping

It is wise to get your Labradoodle microchipped and a legal requirement in some states. Microchipping your dog is a way of being able to permanently identify him, as long as you keep your details up to date with the microchip company.

A microchip is a small metal chip, about the size of a grain of rice, which is inserted under a dog's skin in between the shoulder blades. A veterinarian can insert it in a matter of seconds using a large needle. Your Labradoodle is likely to feel a sharp prick momentarily, but the discomfort then disappears very quickly. When a scanner is run over your dog in the region of the microchip, it comes up with the microchip number. This is directly linked to your information in the microchip company's database.

Neutering

Many people differ in their opinions on this subject. However, there are some major advantages to neutering your Labradoodle if you do not plan to breed him or her. Many Labradoodles will, in fact, come with a contract which states they must be neutered to avoid unwanted breeding.

When you neuter a female dog, it is called a spay, or ovariohysterectomy. During the operation, the veterinarian will remove the ovaries, and usually the uterus, however, some vets just remove the ovaries. Regardless of the technique used, the benefits are both the same. For most medium-sized dogs, the incision is a few inches long, in the center of the belly. Some veterinary practices also offer laparoscopic spay procedures, which is done with a camera and very small incisions. The benefit of this is that the recovery time is much quicker, however it does require a longer anesthetic due to the complexity of the surgery.

The main benefits of spaying your dog are that you are eliminating the risk of a potentially life-threatening uterine infection, called pyometra, as

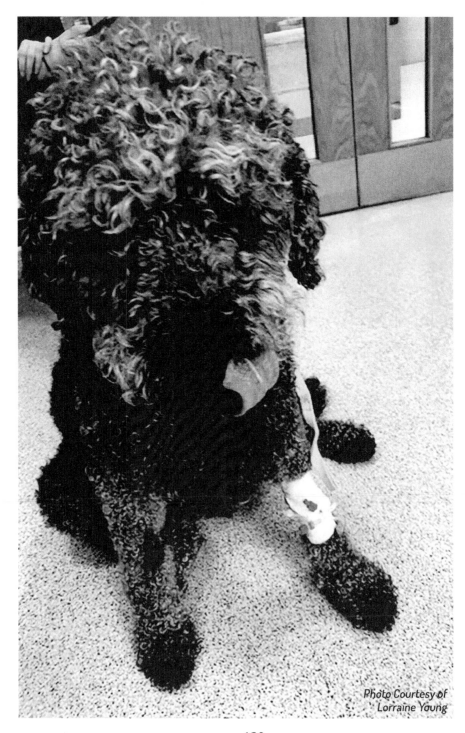

Photo Courtesy of Lorraine Young

well as significantly reducing the chances of mammary cancers. The disadvantage is that by spaying, you can cause the band of muscle which holds the bladder closed, called the urethral sphincter, to loosen, leading to incontinence later. This is because the hormone estrogen helps to tighten this band. You can reduce the chances of this through spaying three months after the first season; however, if you allow the body to experience the reproductive hormones, you slightly increase the risks of mammary cancers.

Castrating a male dog is a less invasive procedure than spaying a female dog. During the operation, both testicles are removed through one incision. Like spaying, there are some major benefits to castrating your dog. It will eliminate the possibility of testicular cancer, and significantly reduce the chances of prostate enlargement or cancer. Also, if done young, it will decrease behavioral issues such as aggression.

Vaccinations

Your first visit to the vet is likely to be when your puppy gets his first vaccination. This can be as young as six weeks old in some cases. Some breeders may take your Labradoodle puppy to get the first vaccination while he is still with them, so he will only need a booster four weeks later.

Vaccinations usually start with a course of two or three injections, followed by yearly boosters. They protect against some very serious canine diseases. If you are hesitant about vaccinating, the most important thing to do is at least take your puppy to have the initial course of two or three injections, and then test his immunity level yearly with a blood titer. That way, you can just give a booster vaccination when the immunity levels drop. However, if you plan to use kennels when you go on vacation, or to insure your dog, you will usually need an up-to-date vaccination card.

The following are diseases which are commonly vaccinated against:

- Distemper = This potentially lethal virus can cause non-specific symptoms, such as sneezing, vomiting, and coughing. It can also cause the hardening and thickening of the pads on the paws and of the nose. It rapidly progresses to death.

- Parvovirus = This virus typically affects young puppies. It causes bloody diarrhea, which is extremely contagious. This gradually causes puppies to weaken due to dehydration and blood loss.

- Leptospirosis = Leptospirosis causes failure of the kidneys and liver, and therefore the most common symptom is yellowing of the gums and eyes, known as jaundice. Some dogs also display neurological symptoms.

- Hepatitis = This is a virus, otherwise known as canine adenovirus. Common symptoms include fatigue, fever, vomiting, diarrhea, and jaundice. Hepatitis can rapidly lead to death.

- Parainfluenza = Parainfluenza is a virus which can lead to a debilitating cough.

- Kennel cough = Kennel cough is highly contagious and causes a honking cough and a fever. This vaccine is squirted up the nose rather than injected.

- Rabies = Rabies is a dangerous disease that causes aggression, hyper-salivation, and neurological symptoms, which lead to death. If a rabid dog bites a human, they also may contract the fatal disease.

Parasite Control

There are many creepy-crawlies which you can find residing in your dog's coat, the most common of which are fleas. Fleas live both in the environment, and on the dog, and feed on your dog's blood. Just because you can't see any fleas, doesn't mean that your dog is not exposed to any, and therefore routinely applying flea treatment as a preventative will help your dog avoid being bitten.

Photo Courtesy of Joe Abkemeier

Many flea treatments also treat other external parasites, such as lice, mites, and ticks, however, you should not assume that every flea treatment will cover all of these. It is important to consider your geographical risks when it comes to parasites. For example, in some areas, such as where there is long grass or lots of wildlife, ticks are very common, whereas dogs living in urban areas are less at risk.

Just as you should routinely treat for external parasites,

you should also routinely treat for internal parasites. These parasites include roundworms and tapeworms.

Some flea treatments also include worming treatments, and so one application will cover all types of parasites, but you should follow your vet's recommendations about what treatments to use on your dog.

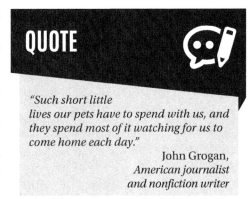

QUOTE

"Such short little lives our pets have to spend with us, and they spend most of it watching for us to come home each day."

John Grogan,
American journalist
and nonfiction writer

Comprehensive worming treatments against roundworms and tapeworms are usually recommended every three months if your dog scavenges, or every six months if he doesn't. Therefore, if your Labradoodle has inherited the appetite of a Labrador, you will certainly have to worm every three months! He won't be able to resist putting his nose to the ground after a scent and gobbling down anything rotten he finds. If you live in an area where lungworms are prevalent, it's best to deworm your dog with a roundworm treatment every month, and then with a tapeworm treatment every three months.

Pet Insurance

Pet insurance will help you deal with any unexpected veterinary costs which may occur, and therefore reduce the worry about a large bill that could hit at any time. Veterinary bills can run into thousands of dollars.

Even if you have insurance, many insurance companies will not cover preventative health care. Items that may fall under this category include vaccinations, external parasite products, de-wormers, grooming products, supplements, and prescription food. The good news is many practices have a 'pet plan' to cover items such as these. It will involve a monthly fee, but included in that are free vaccines and parasite control, and usually discounts on other products.

There are a few different options when it comes to policies; some provide a sum of money which can be spent every year and some provide reimbursement per approved medical treatment. It's important to choose carefully and read the fine print regarding co-pays, conditions that are and aren't covered, etc. Be aware that no pet insurance policy covers pre-existing conditions, so if you plan on obtaining insurance, it's best to do so as soon as possible after you get your dog.

CHAPTER 14
Health

"I have been involved with Labradoodles since 2001. The list of genetic issues that are possible are as many as you see in the Poodle and Retriever parent breeds. Hip dysplasia, eye issues such as cataracts and progressive retinal atrophy, seizures, cardiac issues, thyroid problems, and the list goes on. A good breeder will test for the most common issues in the line and do their best to prevent them from happening. There are so many polygenic and recessive genes though, that it is impossible to completely breed away from any health issue ever be a potential problem. Families looking to purchase a Labradoodle need to understand there is the potential for many different health issues to occur regardless of the degree of testing a breeder has done. I highly recommend families purchase health insurance on their puppy so that they can easily address any major health issue that may occur, without the stress of financial burden."

Rochelle Woods
Spring Creek Labradoodles

Photo Courtesy of
Courtney Nadeau

Labradoodles can be prone to many diseases, which mainly stem from their Labrador genetics. While not all Labradoodles will go on to develop these diseases, it is worth knowing about them. Early detection will lead to early treatment and the best outcome for all. In this chapter, we will look at a comprehensive, although not exhaustive, list of diseases you should be aware of.

Progressive Retinal Atrophy

"Hip dysplasia and retinal eye disease can be of concern. Finding a quality breeder with health testing all through their breeding lines is essential to get a puppy with the best health start possible. By proper health testing breeders can't prevent everything, but can give your new puppy the best possible chance at a long and healthy life with you."

Robby Gilliam
Mountain View Labradoodles

The retina is a structure at the back of the eye which is vital for sight. It's made up of millions of cells called rods and cones. These detect low-level and bright light and convert the light into signals to the brain for processing. Once in the brain, it forms an image.

With Progressive Retinal Atrophy (PRA), the retina's cells begin to die early in life. This means that sight is gradually lost. It's a slow process whereby the rods tend to deteriorate first. This leads to night blindness initially, before the cones also deteriorate and the dog becomes fully blind.

PRA cannot be reversed, so buying a puppy from a breeder who has tested the parents for PRA is your best chance at having a PRA-free Labradoodle. If your Labradoodle has unfortunately begun to develop PRA, then teaching him commands to help him navigate is essential. These are further detailed in Chapter 15.

Luxating Patella

The patella, also known as the kneecap, sits in a groove in the stifle joint. Normally it moves smoothly up and down this groove as the leg extends and flexes, however when one side of the groove is not high enough,

it can slip out of place. This is called a luxation. Most patella luxations are toward the inside of the leg and slip back into place easily. They tend not to cause any pain, as long as the patella does not get stuck outside of the groove; however, they can lead to arthritis of the joint over the years.

Patella luxation can be treated with surgery to either deepen the groove or increase the sides. The procedure is not without risk, as post-operative infections can be catastrophic, but generally, the results are excellent.

Hip and Elbow Dysplasia

"Hip dysplasia is the most prevalent genetic disorder in Labradoodles, I believe. This can be curbed by making sure both parents have had OFA Hip Certifications. A good breeder should readily provide those."

Jenny Williams
Happy Go Lucky Labradoodles

Joint dysplasia of the hip or elbow is a common condition in large-breed dogs, and Labradors are one of the most prone to the condition. The hip is a ball and socket joint where the head of the femur (ball) fits into a socket in the pelvis. Normally this should be a perfect match, like pieces of a puzzle, but when a dog has hip dysplasia either the ball or the socket is malformed. When the shapes don't match well, it means the joint is less stable when it moves. In severe cases of hip dysplasia, the ball can luxate out of the hip socket as it moves, resulting in a wobbly, swaying gait if viewed from behind.

Elbow dysplasia, on the other hand, has many different elements to it. It's not as simple a joint as the hip, and within the elbow dysplasia condition, there can be multiple abnormalities in development. The most common issue in elbow dysplasia is osteochondrosis dissecans (OCD). This is when a flap of joint cartilage separates from the surface. In addition to this, several projections can become detached. These are known as an ununited anconeal process (UAP) and a fragmented medial coronoid process (FMCP). This ultimately leads to lameness or an unusual gait.

Joint dysplasia is usually diagnosed based on X-rays or arthroscopy; however, most veterinarians can determine that a dog is likely suffering from either hip or elbow dysplasia with a simple clinical examination. Joint dysplasia is an inherited condition, and therefore it is usually diagnosed from a young age. X-rays can confirm dysplasia as soon as a dog is fully grown. It is best to understand whether a dog has dysplasia or not from a young age, as if it goes undetected then arthritis will set in at an early stage. This can be mitigated with lifestyle changes, such as keeping your dog controlled on

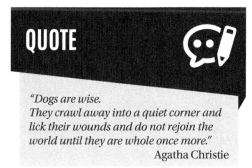

QUOTE

"Dogs are wise. They crawl away into a quiet corner and lick their wounds and do not rejoin the world until they are whole once more."
Agatha Christie

Photo Courtesy of
Amy Miller

walks with minimal jumping, and physical therapies, such as hydrotherapy, to build up muscle. Joint supplements also aid in maintaining joint health. The weight of a dog also plays a big role, as a lighter dog will have less gravitational force on the joints, and therefore less stress. Inevitably, all dogs with joint dysplasia will one day get arthritis; the aim is to avoid this for as long as possible.

For severe cases of both elbow and hip dysplasia, surgery is an option. In elbow dysplasia, surgery usually involves the removal of bone or cartilage fragments. Sometimes a UAP can be reattached with the use of screws if surgery is done at a very young age. With hip dysplasia, the hip joint can be modified by removing the head of the femur, reshaping it and replacing it, or taking it out completely. With both hip and elbow dysplasia, total joint replacement is the gold standard surgical treatment, but implants are expensive.

Prevention is always better than cure, and therefore buying a puppy from a breeder who has had the parents' joints X-rayed and scored is your best bet for a healthy dog. Hip and elbow scoring can be done through the British Kennel Club in the UK and PennHIP at the University of Pennsylvania in the US.

Von Willebrand Disease

Von Willebrand disease is a disorder of the blood. In the blood is a substance called Von Willebrand factor, which aids in the clotting process when your Labradoodle gets cut. If a dog has Von Willebrand disease, then the main symptom is prolonged bleeding. This may be evident as bleeding gums, excessive bleeding when in heat, bleeding from the nose, and constant oozing of blood during surgical procedures.

Von Willebrand is a young dog's disease, and it will be apparent in most before the age of five. It's diagnosed with a blood test; however, clotting times are usually assessed first with a buccal bleeding time test which requires a small prick on the inside of the lip, followed by timing to see how long it takes to stop bleeding.

Unfortunately, there is no cure, but Von Willebrand factor can be transfused, so if a surgical procedure has to be performed, then a preemptive transfusion can mitigate a great deal of bleeding.

Most dogs with Von Willebrand disease can live a normal life, but extra care must be taken to apply pressure to any cuts, as well as not to cut nails too short and cause them to bleed.

Bloat

Bloat is a dangerous condition when the stomach fills up with gas and can happen to any deep-chested dogs. The Labradoodle gets this condition from its Poodle genetics. Bloat is otherwise known as a gastric dilation. It's commonly followed by twisting of the stomach, known as a gastric dilation volvulus, or GDV. A GDV is a surgical emergency, as not only can gas and food not pass out of the stomach, but the blood supply to the stomach becomes cut off, and the stomach wall can die. It's also extremely uncomfortable, and can lead to heart arrhythmias and damage to the spleen.

A vet can usually diagnose bloat or a GDV easily with an X-ray, although he may also have a strong suspicion based on the shape of the upper part of your Labradoodle's abdomen. If it can't be corrected by passing a stomach tube to relieve the gas, there's no other option but to immediately operate.

There are a few schools of thought about how to prevent bloat, although many of them are not backed up with scientific research. The most common thought is to feed your dog multiple meals per day. It's suspected that one large meal per day increases the risk of bloat and GDV. Also, it's advisable not to exercise your dog immediately after eating, to ensure he doesn't run around with a full stomach. Some people also believe that if your dog eats or drinks too fast, he is more likely to experience bloat. You can slow down eating by means of a 'greedy feeder' bowl. These are bowls with projections which you can scatter the food in between, making it harder for your dog to get. Finally, in some dogs with particularly deep chests, veterinarians will do a preemptive surgery to attach the stomach to the abdominal wall, known as a Gastropexy. This is not usually done as a surgery alone, but rather in conjunction with another surgery being performed, such as being spayed. This is a simple surgery and will prevent the stomach from twisting if it does become bloated.

Addison's Disease

Addison's disease, otherwise known as hypoadrenocorticism, is a disease whereby the adrenal glands don't produce sufficient amounts of cortisol and aldosterone. These hormones are vital for everyday functioning. Cortisol helps the body combat stressful situations, and aldosterone plays a vital role in water and electrolyte balance.

Addison's can cause non-specific symptoms such as lethargy, general weakness, vomiting, diarrhea, increased thirst, shaking, and a slow heart rate. As a result, it can be difficult to diagnose, as many conditions cause these symptoms. If left untreated, it can lead to your dog collapsing, which is an emergency.

Addison's is usually diagnosed through a physical examination and blood tests such as an ACTH-stimulation test. This tests the adrenal gland's response to ACTH. For most Addison's cases, the adrenal gland will not respond to the ACTH, and the cortisol level will stay low, because the adrenal gland has been destroyed. However, in rare cases, Addison's disease can be caused by a tumor in the pituitary gland, which produces ACTH to tell the adrenals to work. Therefore, in this case, the adrenals will respond to the blood test.

Addison's disease cannot be cured; however, it can be very well managed by providing replacement cortisol and aldosterone in the form of daily medication.

Cushing's Disease

Cushing's disease is the exact opposite of Addison's disease and is known as hyperadrenocorticism. This occurs when the adrenal glands are overactive. There are two main causes of Cushing's disease, and both are related to your Labradoodle developing tumors. The most common tumor (85 percent of all cases) is one relating to the pituitary gland in the brain. This causes the pituitary to overproduce ACTH, which tells the adrenal glands to produce more cortisol. These tumors are usually small and benign and don't grow enough to cause neurological symptoms. The other type of tumor is one of the adrenal gland itself. These can be benign or malignant and can be surgically removed to cure the disease.

A dog with Cushing's disease will have non-specific clinical symptoms, and like Addison's, it can be difficult to diagnose. Common symptoms include increased hunger, drinking, and urination, lethargy, poor skin health, and poor hair coat. In some cases, the dog might develop a potbellied appearance because fat begins to be deposited in the internal organs, especially the liver, which stretches the abdominal wall.

Cushing's disease is diagnosed through a series of blood tests, as well as a clinical examination. An ACTH stimulation test and a low-dose dexamethasone suppression (LDDS) test are the two most commonly used. A urine test to measure the cortisol:creatinine ratio may also be required.

As mentioned earlier, if the condition is caused by an adrenal tumor, surgery can be curative, but in most cases, lifelong medication will be required. However, many dogs do extremely well on this medication and live a relatively normal life.

Photo Courtesy of
Jennifer Lehman

Epilepsy

Epilepsy causes seizures, but not all seizures are caused by epilepsy. It's something that many people get confused about. Epilepsy is an inherited condition that causes seizures, even though there is nothing structurally wrong with the brain. A seizure happens when the neurons in the brain become hyper-excitable, and all send impulses at the same time.

An epilepsy seizure will start with your Labradoodle just acting a bit strange. He might seek you out, or act more needy than usual. This is called the pre-ictal phase, and may only start a few minutes before the seizure, or even up to an hour beforehand. Then when your dog has a seizure, every animal is different, but common symptoms are shaking of some sort, ranging from slight tremors to convulsions, salivating, urination and/or defecation, and stiff limbs. It's important not to touch your dog at this time, as you could get accidentally bitten. Instead, ensure he is in a safe place, and move away anything surrounding him which might cause harm. It is a good idea to check the time, as if a seizure goes on for more than five minutes, it can be very dangerous to the oxygen levels in his brain. Most seizures won't last much more than a minute, but if it becomes prolonged, you should rush him to your veterinarian. After the seizure, there is a post-ictal phase, which is when your dog might exhibit strange behavior again. This usually lasts from a few hours up to a day or two.

There are medications available which your vet can prescribe to help decrease the frequency of seizures. Regular blood tests will be required to monitor your dog's underlying health, as the medications can damage the liver. However, most are well tolerated. In some cases, your vet may also dispense rectal diazepam to help you stop the seizure early on when it happens.

Hereditary Cataracts

A cataract is when the lens in the eye begins to become opaque, and stops light from being able to hit the back of the eye to be processed by the brain. Whereas most dogs are susceptible to developing cataracts at an elderly age, hereditary cataracts can begin to develop in the first few months of life and lead to complete vision loss by two to three years old.

Luckily, hereditary cataracts are a recessive gene, and therefore both the parents must have the gene for the offspring to develop cataracts. Carriers of the gene, which have one healthy gene and one cataract gene, will not go on to develop cataracts, but regardless they should not be bred from. A genetic test can be done before breeding to ascertain if one of the parents carries the gene.

Cataracts are not painful, and therefore many owners just choose to leave them and live with a blind dog. Many dogs do exceptionally well blind, as long as you don't move furniture around in the house and ensure you keep them on a leash for walks.

For owners who wish to treat their Labradoodle's cataracts, whole lens replacements are a surgical option. It is a complicated and fiddly surgery, and therefore it's only performed by veterinary ophthalmologists.

Atopic Dermatitis

Skin allergies can be due to food, the environment, or bites. When your dog has a flare-up, he will be extremely itchy and may scratch and lick various parts of his body such as his feet, underarms, belly, and the inside of his hind legs. He may also have a flare-up of his ear canals and shake his head excessively to relieve his itchy ears.

If you're treating your dog regularly to prevent external parasites, then the allergy is unlikely to be due to these. However, they should be ruled out with a veterinary examination. A flea allergy only needs one bite to cause your dog to be itchy.

Food allergies should be ruled out with an elimination diet. These are available from your veterinarian. These diets have had all the protein molecules hydrolyzed, which means the body can't recognize them and react. This diet should be fed for six weeks, with no treats or table scraps. If your dog has significantly improved, then different flavors of meat should gradually be introduced again to see what causes the allergy to flare up.

If both parasites and food allergies have been ruled out, the remaining cause is the environment. This could be due to contact with an allergen, such as floor cleaner or long grass, or inhalant, such as pollen. These allergies are difficult to get on top of as they cannot be avoided. There are several treatment options, which focus on three things; treat flare-ups, prevent future flare-ups, and maintain the health of your dog's coat. Allergies cannot be cured.

There are several different tablets available from your vet to aid the itchiness. Steroids are by far the cheapest, but have major side effects as well as putting a lot of strain on the liver. Other options downregulate the immune response to the allergens, but they are costlier.

Another option is for your veterinarian to formulate a vaccination against the allergen. This is administered in increasing intervals, so for example two days apart, then four, then a week, etc. These are effective for many dogs; however, the response is not instant.

Finally, diets containing omega-3 and omega-6 should complement any therapy. In the right ratio, they have pronounced anti-inflammatory effects. They also help build up the lipid layer of the skin to provide a better barrier against external allergens.

Ear Infections

"Labradoodles with small ear canals can be prone to ear infections."

Jenny Walters
Blessings Labradoodles

Labradoodles can be prone to ear canal infections, known as otitis externa. If left untreated, this can spread to the middle ear and cause more complications. This is because since the pinna (flap) of the ear folds down, it creates a warm and moist environment within the ear, which is perfect for yeast and bacteria to grow in. In Chapter 12, we discussed the importance of ear cleaning, especially after swimming, and this certainly will help reduce the likelihood of an infection.

If your Labradoodle does contract an ear infection, he will likely show signs such as shaking his head and scratching his ears. If it progresses to a more serious infection of the middle ear, you might notice a head tilt or loss of balance. Ear infections are extremely sore and can be serious, therefore it is important that you take your Labradoodle to a vet promptly. He will likely need medicated ear drops. If it has progressed to a middle ear infection, he might be admitted for an ear flush instead or be given oral treatment.

The different conditions which your Labradoodle is prone to may seem overwhelming. However, if you purchase a well-bred Labradoodle from a reputable breeder, you will significantly reduce the chances of him being in ill health.

CHAPTER 15
Old Age

If you've been blessed with a long lifetime with your Labradoodle, or have adopted an older dog, you have the privilege and responsibility of guiding him through his senior years. With old age comes increased risks of some conditions, and a requirement to change some things about your dog's lifestyle. By making these changes, you have the best chance of ensuring your Labradoodle lives out his golden years in as healthy a manner as possible. In this chapter, we will look at things to consider in the senior years of your Labradoodle's life, and what you can expect.

Senior Health Checks

When your Labradoodle was younger, you were probably accustomed to taking him to the vet once a year for an annual check-up and vaccination. When your dog reaches the age of eight years old, these annual examinations will change slightly, to become senior health checks. They may happen once a year, or every six months, depending on whether your Labradoodle is struggling with any issues.

A senior health check will start with a general check-up. Your veterinarian will first check the teeth. These can become covered in tartar over time, and may lead to gingivitis as discussed in Chapter 12. Next, your vet will check the eyes for any degenerative processes, such as cataracts, nuclear sclerosis, and retinal degeneration. The next stage of the examination is important; your vet will check the internal organs. He will listen to the heart and the lungs, as well as feel the abdomen for enlargement of the organs or internal masses, which may indicate signs of cancer; something more common in older dogs than younger ones. After this, your vet is likely to do some more in-depth checks. Taking your dog's blood pressure will check that his kidneys and heart are working effectively, and a general blood test will check the health of his internal organs.

While a senior health check may seem a little pricey, comprehensive checks at this age could save you money in the long run. Catching underlying health issues early is really important to ensure that your Labradoodle has a very healthy, long life.

*Photo Courtesy of
Jo Loman*

Senior Nutrition

"A diet rich in protein is essential for their optimal function."

Robby Gilliam
Mountain View Labradoodles

A senior dog requires senior dog food. This is important for your Labradoodle, as in his old age he will require a change in his nutrition. Any reputable dog food brand will have life-stage-appropriate foods.

An older dog is likely to be slower than a younger dog. This is particularly true for Labradoodles, who are prone to joint issues from an early age, as discussed in Chapter 14. Decreased mobility leads to increased weight, especially if your Labradoodle still has a decent Labrador-like appetite! Keeping your dog's weight down will benefit him in the long run as excess weight can put a strain on the heart, liver, and joints. Senior food will have slightly fewer calories, to help your dog maintain a more appropriate weight for his life-stage.

Senior dog foods will also usually have more omega oils in them. These are usually provided through natural ingredients such as fish or oily seeds, like flaxseed. Omega oils are important for your senior Labradoodle and have many benefits. Firstly, they work similarly to anti-inflammatories. If something is inflamed, for example, an arthritic joint, the body will release prostaglandins, specifically PGE2. Omega oils interfere with this chemical pathway and cause the body instead to release PGE3, which is less inflammatory than PGE2. Therefore, this helps decrease the inflammation in sore joints or any inflammatory process. Omega oils also keep the joints, skin, heart, brain, and eyes healthy; many of which are prone to degeneration in your dog's senior years.

Organ Deterioration

While they may not have a specific disease or condition, some organs just don't work as efficiently later in life. Therefore, as mentioned previously, senior wellness checks will monitor the health of the major organs, and if done routinely, will pick up issues at an early stage. If caught early, these can usually be treated with a change in diet, supplements, medication, or some lifestyle changes.

Photo Courtesy of
Debbie Allsopp

HELPFUL TIP
Behavior Changes

As your dog's closest companion, you may be the first to detect changes to your dog's health. While most pet owners are familiar with obvious signs of illness or distress, many do not know that changes in behavior can be an early indicator of disease. Particularly as your dog ages, it's important to keep track of behavioral changes such as sleep pattern changes, increased barking or vocalizing, irritability, or increased accidents in the home. If you notice a change in behavior, talk to your vet.

Sometimes, in older dogs, the valves inside the heart can become leaky. This can lead to some backflow and congestion. Symptoms include listlessness, fainting, coughing, and getting out of breath easily. Starting heart medication early will reduce the pressure on the heart and significantly increase your dog's life span.

Alongside the heart lie the lungs. Usually, the lung tissue is fairly elastic, which allows it to expand and contract as air is breathed in and out. An older dog's lungs become more fibrous with age, they don't expand as well. This might also lead to an inability to fight off infections.

In the abdomen are several organs, such as the stomach, intestines, kidneys, liver, and spleen. Of these, the liver and kidneys are the most prone to age-related deterioration. Both of these organs are involved in filtering out waste products. Therefore, you are doing your dog a great service if you have fed him a good quality diet all of his life, as it means that the body will have made optimum use of the nutrients, filtering out fewer waste products. The liver is also involved in the metabolism of medications, breaking them down into usable forms. This is important to consider when giving older dogs medications, as they may not be able to handle certain ones. Both liver and kidney deterioration or failure only show signs when they are advanced, which is why it is important to pick them up early with routine senior blood tests. This will give your dog the best prognosis possible. Symptoms you may notice are weight loss, vomiting, loss of appetite, and a general sluggish demeanor.

Loss of Senses

Loss of the senses will not affect your dog medically or shorten his life span, but it may affect his quality of life to some degree.

The most common senses to deteriorate are hearing and sight. Luckily, it is very rare for a dog to lose his sense of smell, which is good as your Lab-

Photo Courtesy of Eileen Hawkins

radoodle is likely to love running around with his nose to the ground, picking up all sorts of scents.

Surprisingly, dogs do extremely well without sight. If blindness happens suddenly, it may take your dog a while to adjust, however, if it is gradual, many owners don't even realize that their dogs have lost, or partially lost, their vision. The most common reasons why dogs lose their sight are cataracts, and retinal degeneration. Most elderly dogs will develop nuclear sclerosis in their lenses, which can look like cataracts. But the cloudiness that it creates is not opaque, and your dog will still have some vision. If your Labradoodle begins to lose his sight, then teaching him to cope early on is a good idea. Labradoodles are very smart and can learn new commands even in old age. Teaching commands such as 'slowly,' 'wait,' 'turn,' and 'stop' will prevent him from getting into trouble. He will also be able to navigate his way around the house with ease, as long as you keep the furniture in the same place, as his memory of navigating special areas will still be excellent.

Photo Courtesy of Nigel Holmes

For dogs that have experienced a total loss of vision, a product known as a 'Halo' or 'Bumper Collar' is available. This is a flexible hoop that attaches to a harness, encircling the dog's head. It will make contact with any obstacles before your dog bumps into them, and can greatly improve the confidence of a blind dog.

Hearing loss, though, is a sense that is slightly more difficult to manage. When you teach your dog commands as a puppy, always combine a voice command with a signal. That way, if your dog loses some or all of his hearing, he can still understand you. Hearing loss is usually gradual, and it is likely that you will not realize your dog is losing his hearing until it is quite advanced. You may even think it's the stubbornness of the Poodle coming through and that he is ignoring you! Unfortunately, there is nothing that can be done to regenerate your Labradoodle's hearing, but he can still live a happy life without it, although as his recall will be affected, he will need to be kept on the leash near hazards such as traffic, cliff edges, or livestock.

Arthritis

It's very common for elderly dogs to develop arthritis. Approximately 20 percent of all dogs over the age of eight suffer from the condition. This is an average across all dog breeds, and unfortunately, Labradoodles and Labradors are significantly over-represented in that 20 percent. Because of this, starting your dog on joint supplements before arthritis sets in is important.

The moving joint comprises of six components; the joint capsule, the cartilage, the subchondral bone (under the cartilage), the ligaments and tendons, the nerves and blood vessels, and the synovial fluid filling the joint. All six components are involved in arthritis.

The joint capsule is made up of two layers. The outer layer is dense and fibrous, and its purpose is to protect the inner layer. The inner layer membrane produces a substance called hyaluronic acid which makes up the synovial fluid. It is richly supplied with blood vessels and has plenty of nerve endings. This means it detects pain very well.

The cartilage is composed of cells called chondrocytes, molecules called glycosaminoglycans, and collagen fibers. It doesn't have many blood vessels or nerves, and therefore its nutrients come from the synovial fluid and subchondral bone. Its function is as a shock absorber for the joint, due to the great amount of water it holds. It also provides a smooth surface to allow the joint to glide. Unfortunately, cartilage cannot regenerate once damaged.

Photo Courtesy of Beverley Roberts

The synovial fluid is a transparent or pale-yellow protein-rich fluid, comprised of hyaluronic acid. The functions of the synovial fluid are to allow for constant load-bearing, efficient heat conductivity, and lubrication.

When a joint has arthritis, the cartilage gradually deteriorates and the subchondral bone becomes thick, reducing the shock-absorbing capacity of the joint. Also, the inner membrane becomes thickened, and the surrounding areas become devitalized because of the reduction in blood supply. The thick inner membrane grows into the joint space and starts to become stuck to the cartilage. As a result, the synovial fluid can no longer flow normally into the pores of the cartilage, leading to deceased nutrition and degeneration.

In a nutshell, the joint becomes very sore and loses a great amount of function. When people think of arthritis, they think of limping. And that certainly is the main symptom which is seen. However, by the time your Labradoodle is limping, he may already have moderate or severe arthritis, so it's vital to look out for early indications of pain.

There are some tell-tale signs to look out for, which even stoic dogs will demonstrate if they're in pain. The first sign is a change in breathing. Dogs in pain generally breathe at a faster rate. This can be shallow, or it can be panting. It's easy to mistake this for your dog feeling hot or worn out, but it should not be forgotten that pain often causes this symptom. There can also be behavior changes. These can be changes like increased aggression, avoiding affection, reacting when picked up, or generally being quieter than usual. If the pain gets very bad, your Labradoodle may struggle to settle. Lying down in a comfortable position can be a struggle for a dog in pain. You are likely to see him circle round and round before lying down, and once he's down, it won't be long before he's up again. Another common sign is licking the sore area, possibly obsessively. Dogs find comfort in licking areas of pain. You may not see him actively licking, but orange or brown saliva stains over the joints are an indication that he is secretly doing it. Finally, your dog may have difficulty passing stools. If he suffers from either back or hip pain, squatting to pass stools can be very uncomfortable. He may avoid going potty because of the pain, and as a result, become constipated, or he may get into an awkward position to do his business.

Your vet can easily diagnose arthritis by checking the joints for a feeling called crepitus. This is a creaking that can be felt when manipulating the joints. He may wish to do X-rays to confirm the extent of the arthritis, however, often this is not necessary for a diagnosis.

Arthritis is best managed with a multimodal approach. This means that by using multiple different strategies concurrently, you will get the best result.

Most owners expect their vet to prescribe anti-inflammatories as the mainstay of treatment, and this is certainly important to improve your dog's comfort. However, many anti-inflammatories can have serious side effects on the gut, liver, and kidneys, so routine blood tests to check that the organs can handle medications are vital to do on a yearly basis.

The next thing to add to your dog's treatment is a good quality supplement. There are plenty on the market, and it can be difficult to determine which are good quality and which are not. Generally, you will get what you pay for, so if you buy something cheap, it is not likely to be of good quality. You should look out for ingredients such as glucosamine hydrochloride (not sulfate), chondroitin sulfate, MSM, hyaluronic acid, and omega oils (DHA and EPA, or omega-3 and omega-6). Some might also contain green-lipped mussel. These ingredients help to maintain the joint fluid, for improved lubrication, and aid in building up the cartilage where it has been damaged. They will never fix arthritis, but they help to slow down the disease progression.

Finally, treating arthritis with complementary therapies will help improve your Labradoodle's comfort and fitness. Complementary therapies should be just that; complementary. They are not designed to use instead of medications, but they help in conjunction with conventional treatment. Examples of therapies include physiotherapy, chiropractic therapy, hydrotherapy, and acupuncture. These improve comfort, but more importantly fitness, as this is something that tends to deteriorate when a dog is not active due to sore joints.

Saying Goodbye

The final days of your dog's life can be a very emotional time. Sometimes it is clear cut, and other times it may not be so obvious when you should make the decision. But regardless of the situation, your vet will be able to advise you about the health of your dog and whether his quality of life is compromised. When it comes to quality of life, there are three questions you should consider: Does your Labradoodle still want to eat? Does he still wag his tail and seem happy at times? And does he still interact with you? If his condition causes you to answer no to those questions, and nothing more can be done to improve his well-being, then it might be time to consider putting him to sleep.

The injection will be done by your veterinarian, and while it is a sad time, it is usually a very peaceful procedure. Your veterinarian may start by sedating your Labradoodle, and then placing a catheter in the vein in his leg. Once you've said your goodbyes, an overdose of anesthetic is given. This is not painful and causes the brain to go into a deep sleep before stopping the heart. It only takes a matter of seconds. Your vet will check the heart to confirm your dog has passed away. The injection can be given at home, at the vet practice, or in your car. The important thing is that it is done somewhere that your dog will feel calm.

Saying goodbye is always hard, but in the end, it's an act of love that you can peacefully end your dog's suffering. While you're bound to feel sad about the loss of your companion, you should try to find comfort in remembering all the wonderful times that you had with your Labradoodle, and how much joy he brought you over the years.

Printed in Great Britain
by Amazon